# TANGY
# TART
# HOT &
# SWEET

## A WORLD OF RECIPES FOR EVERY DAY

# TANGY TART HOT & SWEET

## A WORLD OF RECIPES FOR EVERY DAY

**PADMA LAKSHMI**

ART DIRECTION AND DESIGN BY ERIKA OLIVEIRA
PHOTOGRAPHY BY DITTE ISAGER
ADDITIONAL PORTRAIT PHOTOGRAPHY BY CHARLES THOMPSON

WEINSTEIN BOOKS

Food Stylist Susie Theodorou
Prop Stylist Robyn Glaser
Photos of Padma Lakshmi on pages 51, 93, 103, 202, and 237 by Charles Thompson.
Photos of Padma Lakshmi and Alice Temperley on page 103 courtesy of wireimage.

Printed in the United States of America. For information address
Weinstein Books, 99 Hudson Street, New York, NY 10013

ISBN: 978-1-60286-006-3
ISBN 10: 1-60286-006-8

First Edition
10  9  8  7  6  5  4  3  2  1

# ACKNOWLEDGMENTS

Jin Auh

Pippa Beng

Frances Berwick

Allison Binder

Anthony Bonsignore

Banu Chidambaram

Andrew Cohen

Tom Colicchio

Katie Finch

Susan Friedland

Robyn Glaser

Gerry Greenberg

Ofelia Guieb

Judy Hottensen

Ditte Isager

Rajilakshmi Krishnamurthi

Vijaya Lakshmi

Shauna Minoprio

Manu Nathan

Erika Oliveira

Adrian Palacios

Christina Papadopoulos

Kristin Powers

Peter Prasad

Eric Ripert

Milan Rushdie

Salman Rushdie

Zafar Rushdie

Rick Schwartz

Frank Selvaggi

Dave Serwatka

Gail Simmons

Doug Stone

Neela Subramanian

Susie Theodorou

Charles Thompson

Tamara Tohill

Christian Vesper

Franca Virgigli

Harvey Weinstein

Rob Weisbach

Jutta Weiss

Andrew Wylie

Lauren Zalaznick

And the countless others who helped in ways big and small.

*For S. R.*

# CONTENTS

There is a communion of more than
our bodies when bread is broken and
wine is drunk. —M.F.K. Fisher

When I was a little girl, my mother worked full time and then went to classes several nights a week for her master's degree. I would often help her in the kitchen when she got home. It was where we spent the most hours together. I graduated from shelling peanuts and breaking off the ends of beans to chopping vegetables and standing at the stove. My mother, who is a great cook, was famous for being able to make an impromptu meal in half an hour with whatever she had in the kitchen at the time. She was known for being able to whip something up out of nothing. I learned at her elbow and watched. In those days it was harder to find black mustard seeds, fresh ginger, and coconut milk. But she'd use whatever she found, whatever she tasted in other peoples' homes, and she'd bring home some strange flora from the farmer's market that would find its way into a pot, bubbling away with a bit of seasoning. Before you knew it a whole meal was being placed hot and steaming on the table while you were just chatting by the stove. She had a gift for making everyone feel welcome, and everything so easy. You would want to drop in on her; she'd make you want to come back again and again. That's what a good hostess does when you're at her table.

Being a single mom gave my mother little opportunity to linger in the kitchen for hours, and so as I stood by her side I too learned to improvise and make things taste good in a rush. She was, and still is, great at simplifying all sorts of exotic dishes. In New York, where we'd moved to start a new life, there were immigrants like us from all over the world, and our kitchen was heavily influenced by them.

From Polish sausages to Vietnamese steamed fish, the world was right here on our island. I had a Peruvian babysitter named Elena who taught me how to make mashed potato empanadas. Otis, my mom's boyfriend at the time, was from Barbados. Through him we experienced the tropical curries of the Caribbean. My playmates from one floor down were Filipino, and at their mother's table I tasted the noodle dish pancit.

The dishes we tasted throughout the city, in restaurants, at other people's houses, in the sharing of packed lunches at school and work—all made their way into our kitchen. We went to the Puerto Rican market in Spanish Harlem for sugarcane. We frequented Chinatown to buy salted plums and bok choy. My mother never missed an opportunity to introduce my young palate to new and surprising tastes.

When I was older, we moved to a suburb of Los Angeles, and I traveled to India for holidays. I used to stop along the way in Singapore and Tokyo. These trips broadened my culinary horizons even more. By the time I was in college I was trying different recipes from the international students who cooked in my dorm. When I studied abroad in Spain, the first things I learned to say in Spanish were the names of the ingredients I needed to make the dishes that reminded me of home. Later I learned to duplicate in my own kitchen what I had tasted in Madrid's vast array of restaurants and tapas bars.

My career as a model took me around the globe, and I continued my gastronomical research every place I went. Living in Paris, I learned about European food traditions to which I had never been exposed. I learned that the Spanish, French, and Italian all use béchamel sauce in various dishes. When I lived in Milan, I absorbed as much of the region's gastronomy as I could. Then living and working in Rome taught me about southern Italian cuisine. I realized that French food was actually based on pre-Columbian Italian cuisine; Catherine de' Medici married the future French king Henri II and took her Florentine culinary practices with her to France. It wasn't until the tomato was introduced from the New World that Italian food became as different from its French counterpart as it now is.

Making movies took me to Cuba and Sri Lanka, where I began to see the connections between South American and Asian food. Mangoes and coconuts, cumin, coriander (cilantro), and tamarind were cropping up in all sorts of cuisines. The world of food seemed to be getting bigger and smaller at the same time.

Eating and cooking is as much about our identity as about our mood. I believe the American palate is the most open and inviting audience for the world's flavors. The best thing about an immigrant culture is the choice and variety of tastes and ingredients it offers. One would be a fool not to sample the myriad exotic (and now not so exotic) dishes there are to enjoy.

Most Americans can trace their roots to an Old World connection, and our grandmothers jealously guard their treasure troves of recipes from their particular ethnic ancestry. Add to those passed-down recipes a selection from one's partner or spouse's family, then mix those with dishes gathered from travel and recipes traded between friends, and it's easy to see why you don't have to be a world traveler to have an eclectic palate. The world now comes to you, on every street corner and in every food court.

When I look at how Americans eat today, I come to the conclusion that we are all a little bit Chinese, a little bit Mexican, a little bit Italian and French. No one I know eats one type of cuisine all the time. Our lives have all been touched by the many cultures that coexist among us. The way we eat now is a reflection of what America has become.

My identity can be very accurately traced through my fork. I grew up first in South India, and the roots of many of my recipes are there. Starting out with a few chilies, some mustard seeds, and ginger, I was able to learn the secrets of my grandmother's kitchen. Most of my fondest early memories are of being with my mother, my aunts, and my grandmother in the kitchen. I came to equate cooking with celebration, and food with love.

Most of us do not eat a single cuisine all the time, or indeed even for all of one week. Whenever we celebrate anything, a birth, a marriage, a death, when we court each other, for business or friendship or romance, what do we do? We eat. What do we eat? All kinds of things. One day sushi, another Thai, a third Italian, and the fourth day . . . maybe Mexican, or how about Moroccan?

I cook the way I eat. I love fresh ingredients, clean flavors that stand out on their own, and healthy dashes of some unexpected spice that give a dish originality. The only recipes I remember are ones that arouse passionate and emotional responses in me. I want to eat a rice dish that transports me to the paddies of Indonesia, a couscous dish to remind me of mysterious Marrakech, and a fiery curried broth to evoke my lost childhood in the deep lushness of the South Indian rain forest. Like most of us, I have been influenced by the people around me. A Peruvian babysitter, a Korean college roommate, an Italian lover, and a Swiss aunt have all affected my cooking, and I am grateful to them for making my life in the kitchen more robust and complicated. I can think of no better pleasure than to be near a hot stove and a chopping block full of things waiting to be made into something that can be gathered around, savored, and enjoyed with people I want to spend time with. That's really why we cook—to make others happy, to share with them the most human, the most intimate function of life: to eat.

The recipes in this book reflect how my generation eats: a little of this and a little of that. It spans many ethnicities and food traditions because that's who we are, today, as a culture. More than ever we are a nation of adventurers, at least with our forks. We are also a nation with very little time on our hands. But we do want to impress those we love with luscious flavors and sumptuous colors that cater to the senses and fill our bellies with happiness. We want simple recipes for complex flavors. These recipes meet those standards. I recommend doing all the chopping before starting so that all the ingredients are ready at hand. I also encourage the cook to taste the dish often and play with the recipes, tailoring them to his or her own palate. And most of all, remember to cook with your heart, because cooking is celebration, and food is love.

# STARTERS & APPETIZERS

# GRILLED CHEESE TOASTIE WITH PORTOBELLO AND BACON

Sometimes the best recipes are born as a result of clearing the fridge. I was doing just this when I had a handful of mushrooms left over and a couple of strips of bacon that needed using before I left town. You could use a slice or two of good, honey-baked ham or prosciutto instead for a splendid variation.

2 strips apple-wood-smoked bacon
½ cup chopped portobello mushrooms
2-inch sprig fresh thyme, which yields about
⅛ teaspoon of leaves
2 ½ tablespoons honey
4 teaspoons spicy mustard
4 slices sourdough bread
4 ounces sheep's milk cheese (preferably
Ossato Brebis) cut into ¼-inch-thick pieces
a few pats of butter at room temperature

**1** Heat a frying pan over medium heat. Add the bacon. When cooked well done but not burned, remove and place on a paper towel.

**2** In the same pan, sauté the mushrooms in the bacon fat, adding the fresh thyme after 3 minutes. While the mushrooms are cooking, cut the bacon strips into bite-size pieces, cutting away any excess fat, if necessary. Put the bacon back into the pan with the mushrooms. Cook for 2 to 3 more minutes until the mushrooms are browned, and turn off the heat.

**3** Whisk the honey and mustard together in a small bowl to make a thick sauce.

**4** Thinly spread the honey-mustard sauce on one side of each slice of bread. Then cover 2 of the slices with the cheese, making sure to cover the entire surface. Spread the bacon and mushroom mixture over the cheese.

**5** Place the other 2 slices of bread on top, and butter the outsides of each sandwich. Place the sandwiches in a frying pan and cover.

**6** Cook on medium-low heat for 5 to 6 minutes until the bottom sides are golden brown. Then carefully flip the sandwiches over with a spatula, cover, and cook for another 3 minutes. In the last few minutes, when you can see the cheese melting on the sides, remove the lid to let out the steam so the sandwiches don't get soggy. Cut the sandwiches into bite-size squares, and serve while still hot. SERVES 4

# KERALAN CRAB CAKES

Who doesn't love crab cakes? I know of no one. I made this recipe to meld a classic American dish with the hot and tangy flavors of my native Kerala. Since crab dishes are abundant in South Indian cuisine, the marriage is a happy one. I liberally use hot green chilies, but they can be reduced a bit to taste. The shredded coconut gives the dish a South Asian twist, and the dried mango powder adds sourness. If you don't happen to have the amchoor, don't despair. Add some lemon juice to the mixture instead. If you do this, you'll probably need less milk. I sometimes use sumac powder as an alternative, too, but more about that later.

1 pound crab meat, shredded
½ cup dry bread crumbs
½ cup flour
8 serrano chilies, minced
1 cup chopped chives
1 cup shredded unsweetened coconut
½ cup shredded carrot
½ cup finely diced celery
1 teaspoon amchoor *
1 cup sweet corn, fresh, canned or
    frozen, drained
1 large egg, beaten
1 teaspoon salt
2 cups (approximately) canola oil, for frying
¼ cup milk
    Fresh Mint Chutney (page 246)

**1** Combine all the ingredients in a mixing bowl except the oil, milk, and chutney. Add the milk a bit at a time; you may need a bit more or less than ¼ cup to adhere the ingredients into a thick cohesive mixture.

**2** Form patties 3 inches in diameter and about 1 inch thick.

**3** Fill a deep skillet with ½ inch of oil and place it over medium heat. Once the oil is hot and simmering (test for readiness by dropping a loose kernel of corn into it—if the oil sizzles and tiny bubbles form around the kernel, the oil is ready), gently fry the patties, turning them over to brown on each side. Do not crowd the pan, and use 2 spatulas to turn.

**4.** Lay the fried patties on a few paper towels to absorb excess oil. Serve hot, with mint chutney on the side. **SERVES 6**

**NOTE** Amchoor is a light, sawdust-brown powder made of sun-dried green mangoes. It's a great souring agent when you don't want to add moisture to a dish. Found at most Indian grocery stores, it will keep in your pantry for ages.

# TEA SANDWICHES WITH LEMON, HONEY, AND GINGER

I first tasted the flavor combination of lemon, honey, and ginger in a very expensive bottle of spread I found at a swanky gourmet shop I like to call a "boutique for food." I'm a sucker for condiments, especially ones that are called things like citron confit au gingembre and adorned with pretty labels that look very Old World. But then I realized I could make them myself at home and actually tweak them to taste . . . well, *better*. Or did I first taste the combination of lemon, honey, and ginger in a Luden's cough drop? No matter, the flavor is out of this world. The happy marriage of lemon and ginger gives a lovely, gentle flavor to these sandwiches. The peppery taste of pecorino is balanced nicely by the sweet taste of honey. It keeps in the fridge in an airtight jar for weeks.

10 slices of good white bread, toasted on both sides
2 preserved lemon halves (sold in
   specialty stores; also see page 112)
2 teaspoons honey
1 teaspoon crushed dried red peppers (see box)
1 tablespoon freshly minced ginger
10 thin slices of a hard Italian cheese like
   pecorino or caciotta

**1** Arrange the toast on a platter.

**2** Chop the preserved lemons, being sure to remove any seeds first. Place them in a processor or blender with the honey, red pepper, and ginger; make a smooth paste.

**3** Spread the paste on the toast and top with a slice of cheese. Diagonally cut each slice to make equal triangles from each slice. You can serve as is or heat in a 350°F oven for a few minutes, just until cheese is melted and toasted. Either way, these are wonderful with tea or, even better, a glass of sherry. SERVES 6–8

## MAKING YOUR OWN CRUSHED RED PEPPER

I once received a wreath of bright red, dried chili peppers as a Christmas gift. While they looked gorgeous hanging in my kitchen, I was anxious not to let them get old and go to waste. So I got it into my head to make my own crushed red pepper. I'd been buying this item for years in jars, but as I thought about it, I realized my foremothers and aunts crushed up peppers for certain dishes. So I took out my stone mortar and, with a pestle, crushed a few. The piquant aroma of the chilies filled me with glorious red heat in the dead of an icy winter. Now I try to crush just a handful at a time once a month rather than use the stale, old, store-bought kind. It really makes a difference. When you do this, be careful not to inhale the red pepper dust that gets kicked up. Chilies can be dangerous.

## HOW TO PEEL A POMEGRANATE

For peeling pomegranates you need to wear an old shirt that you don't mind getting permanently stained. With a sharp paring knife, split the fruit in half, then into quarters; it will bleed red liquid all over, so be sure to use a large cutting board and have paper towels handy to sop up the liquid. Now, with your fingers, gently free the garnet seeds of fruit from the white pith. If you pull opposite ends of the quarter of fruit apart, some will pop out easily, but you will have to carefully remove the white webbed covering. The remaining seeds will be clustered in groups and attached to the white pith. Gently pry them off into a bowl. Make sure there are no white bits clinging to the seeds. If covered, they will keep in the fridge for up to four or five days.

# TEA SANDWICHES WITH GOAT CHEESE AND CUCUMBER

Okay, so most of us don't sit around and have afternoon tea anymore, but these graceful little triangles dotted with garnet jewels of pomegranate and grassy notes of cucumber and dill demand an occasion worthy of them. They can be made so easily and are perfect for whipping up whenever guests descend unexpectedly. I agree most of us don't keep shelled pomegranates in our fridge, but many of the better grocery stores often sell pre-peeled pomegranate seeds near the sliced melon in the produce section. Pomegranates are mostly available in the fall; you can substitute dried cranberries or cherries for them the rest of the year. If the dried berries are large, chop them up into morsels first. The taste is different but just as scrumptious.

10 thin, square slices of good white bread grilled
   or toasted on both sides
¼ teaspoon olive oil
2 ounces goat cheese, about a 2-inch cube
2 to 3 teaspoons dill
   fresh pomegranate seeds (see page 8)
40 ⅛-inch-thick slices of English cucumber,
   approximately half the cucumber

**1** Place the toast on a platter.

**2** Combine the olive oil, goat cheese, and dill. Spread this paste evenly onto the toasts.

**3** Sprinkle with the pomegranate seeds, gently pressing them into the cheese.

**4** Place 4 slices of cucumber on top of the cheese on each slice of toast.

**5** Carefully cut each slice diagonally to make triangles. Ideally two of the four cucumber slices will also be cut in half. These are best served open-face and arranged on a platter. They're great with afternoon tea or to accompany cocktails. **SERVES 4–6**

# MUSHROOM AND GOAT CHEESE FLAUTAS

This is a recipe that everyone loves, especially teenagers. It's a yummy crowd pleaser that's great to make by the platterful for any party. The flautas are best served hot right out of the pan and with plenty of the dipping sauce. The fresh tortillas will keep in the fridge, as will the cheeses, so this is also something you can make spontaneously when a hungry mob shows up.

2 tablespoons extra virgin olive oil
½ cup diced shallots
8 ounces fresh portobello mushrooms, diced
1 teaspoon dried oregano
1 teaspoon dried thyme
1 teaspoon dried dill
½ teaspoon crushed red pepper
   salt
8 ounces feta cheese
4 ounces ricotta cheese
8 8-inch-diameter flour tortillas *
   canola oil, for frying
   Fresh Mint and Date Dipping Sauce (page 246)

**1** Over medium-high heat, heat 2 tablespoons of olive oil in a large skillet. Toss in the shallots and mushrooms, and sauté for 2 minutes. Add the oregano, thyme, dill, and crushed red pepper, and stir for 3 more minutes. Add a sprinkle of salt and sauté for a few minutes, until the mushrooms are browned. Remove from heat.

**2** In a large bowl, combine the feta and ricotta cheeses with the sautéed shallots and mushrooms, mixing well to form a paste.

**3** Lay 1 tortilla flat on a cutting board. Spoon 2 heaping teaspoons of mixture into a line across the tortilla, horizontally, near the side closest to you. Leave about a 1-inch border. Roll the nearest end over the mixture and keep rolling until the tortilla is in the shape of a flute. Press down gently as you roll to distribute the cheese mixture throughout the inside of the flute. Be careful not to push too hard; you don't want it to seep out of the sides. Close the tortilla using a wooden toothpick as a straight pin (not perpendicular, but parallel to the flute) to hold the end of the tortilla shut. Do this with all the tortillas.

**4** Place a skillet filled to a depth of 1 inch with canola oil over medium-high heat. When the oil gets hot (you can test oil with a small piece of tortilla—if it bubbles and sizzles, it's ready), turn the heat down to just lower than medium and fry the flautas on each side until golden brown. This should take no more than 1 to 2 minutes total; turn to brown each side every 30 seconds. When done, immediately place the flautas on paper towels to drain excess oil. When cool enough to touch, carefully ease out the toothpicks before serving. Each flauta can be cut in half on an angle before serving, as they are quite filling . Serve with Fresh Mint and Date Dipping Sauce (page 246). **SERVES 8**

**NOTE** Tortillas at room temperature are softer and easier to pierce and manipulate than cold ones, so take them out of the fridge before starting the recipe.

# HOT AND SOUR FRUIT CHAAT

I am not one to shy away from the stove, but there are times when it's so hot I'd rather stick a needle in my eye than turn it on. This cool appetizer is refreshing, and easy to make. And it's really healthy. I love the flavors in this dish—especially the fresh, sharp, bursting green flavor that comes from mingling sweet, ripe fruit with citrus juices. I use yuzu (a Japanese citrus fruit) juice in this recipe and many others, and I advise everyone to buy a bottle and keep it on hand in the fridge for salad dressings. Add it to anything that normally requires lemon juice. I promise you the bottle will not go to waste. Another of my secret weapons, yuzu adds the clean aroma of lime trees and the ocean to anything. However, you can certainly substitute lime juice if don't have any yuzu around.

The tartness of yuzu juice with plums and apples, paired with the spicy bite of black cumin and cayenne, make this much more glamorous than a typical fruit salad. I usually serve it on a flat platter, arranging the fruit like petals in a colorful flower pattern. If you're serving a buffet, it's nice to cut the fruit into tiny chunks and serve it in juice glasses with spoons to scoop the fruit. You can even pour a shot of ice-cold vodka in it for a naughty start to a great evening. You may find guests asking for seconds. (If you add vodka, remember to leave out the sesame oil in the recipe, as oil and alcohol do not mix well.) If pomegranates are not in season, make this starter without them and it will still be lovely.

1 Granny Smith apple, cored, peeled, and sliced
  into thin crescents
2 large firm black plums, pitted and sliced thinly
1 English cucumber, unpeeled and sliced into
  thin rounds
1 red bell pepper, seeded and cut into long, thin
  strands
1 cup fresh pomegranate seeds
¼ cup chopped fresh mint
1 tablespoon concentrated yuzu juice (available
  at Japanese grocery stores)
1 tablespoon fresh-squeezed lime juice
1 tablespoon toasted sesame oil
½ teaspoon cayenne
1 teaspoon black cumin powder *
coarsely ground sea salt

**1** Decoratively arrange the apple, plums, cucumber, and pepper on a large plate. Or you can arrange the fruit on individual serving plates. Sprinkle with the pomegranate seeds and fresh mint. You can prepare the fruits and vegetables a few hours ahead of serving up to this point. Cover and refrigerate.

**2** Combine all the other ingredients, except the salt, in a bowl and whisk together. This step, too, can be done in advance and the mixture refrigerated until serving time.

**3** Pour the dressing over the fruit and sprinkle with salt. SERVES 4–6

**NOTE** This is a different type of cumin from the more common beige-gray seeds—think of anise seed compared to caraway seed. Its flavor is less pungent, more tart and peppery. It is available at Indian grocery stores, but if you don't have it around, leave it out and the dish will still be a success.

# SAVORY PITA CRISPS DUSTED WITH SUMAC AND SEA SALT

Sumac is a spice powder made from dried, sour, red berries that grow on bushes. It is used throughout the Middle East, and it is thought that both ancient Romans and Native Americans used sumac berries as souring agents. They have a vibrant vermilion color, so sumac adds both a fruity sour flavor and visual richness to any dish. I keep it in my spice rack to dress up fish and vegetables, and even to sprinkle over creamy sauces for added color. This is a secret weapon that is worth its weight in gold. You can serve these crisps by themselves, warm from the oven, or with any dip, such as hummus, or with a simple, fresh, blended chutney like the Fresh Mint and Date Dipping Sauce (page 246). They will keep for a few days in an airtight container or plastic freezer bag. You can make these without sumac too, or try them with some fresh rosemary leaves.

4 large whole pita rounds
¼ cup extra virgin olive oil
½ teaspoon sumac powder
½ teaspoon sea salt

**1** Preheat the oven to 375°F.

**2** Slice the pita into 8 pie-shaped wedges, and tear apart the thick halves from the thin halves. Keep the thick portions separated from the thin ones.

**3** In a bowl, combine ⅛ cup of olive oil and ¼ teaspoon of sumac. Place the thick halves of the pita slices in the bowl and gently toss with your hands, coating all the pieces but being careful not to break them apart. Now grind the sea salt with a mortar and pestle; add ¼ teaspoon to the bowl and toss. Lay these slices out on one half of a baking pan.

**4** Repeat the process with the thinner pita slices, using the same bowl and the other half of the sumac, oil, and sea salt. Remember to add the sea salt only after the oil has soaked into the pita. Arrange these slices on the other half of the baking pan and place in the preheated oven. The thinner pita slices should be crispy enough in 8 to 10 minutes, while the thicker slices will take longer. This is why the two groups are kept separate in the oven: when the thin crisps are ready, remove them and place the thick slices back into the oven for an additional 5 to 8 minutes. SERVES 4

# SMOKED SALMON TIMBALE

This is a great first course when you don't want something spicy, but rather something simple and classic. Because one can find smoked salmon and goat cheese at many corner delis, it's a great dish to whip up on weeknights when you haven't got much time after work before sitting down to dinner. If pomegranates are difficult to find and peel in time, chopped dried cranberries are lovely. Green apples can also be substituted for the pears. Once assembled, the dish looks very elegant, like you've worked much harder than you actually have.

4 ½-cup ramekins *
8 ounces sliced smoked salmon
4 tablespoons pomegranate seeds, with all white
   pith removed (see page 8)
1 8 ounce fresh goat cheese log, sliced into
   8 disks
1 pear, cored and sliced horizontally into thin
   rings
2 cups salad greens
   olive oil and balsamic vinegar (optional)

**1** Line the inside of each ramekin with plastic wrap, making sure there is enough overhang to grab for easy removal.

**2** Cut the slices of the salmon—4 for each mold—into circles and place the first slice neatly on the bottom of the mold. Next, sprinkle a layer of pomegranate seeds over the salmon.

**3** Now layer the goat cheese. Each slice of cheese must first be cut and/or shaped so it will fit the mold. Then place a slice in each mold. If your goat cheese is not in log form, about 1 tablespoon spread evenly should do the trick.

**4** Add the sliced pears—2 slices in each mold. Gently but firmly pack the ingredients with the tips of your fingers; push down on the pear slices so the goat cheese compresses and the ingredients are nicely packed but remain separated in distinct layers. Repeat the layers. Place in the refrigerator for at least 20 minutes.

**5** When ready to serve, turn each mold upside down onto a salad plate. Hold down the edges of the plastic wrap as you lift the ramekin and then remove the plastic wrap. The timbale should be nicely formed. Spread a handful of greens around each timbale to decorate. A bit of olive oil and balsamic vinegar can be tossed with or drizzled on the greens, if desired, but do this just before serving. **SERVES 4**

**NOTE** If ramekins are unavailable, you can use any small, wide-mouthed glass, or even a teacup with a 1-cup capacity. My mother used to open a small can of corn on both top and bottom, wash it thoroughly, and use it as a mold. The plastic wrap makes removal and serving easier.

# LOBSTER BRUSCHETTA

These bruschette are children of the much beloved lobster rolls that are such a favorite along the East Coast. They are very easy to make and quite a bit more decadent than the normal bruschetta of tomato and basil. They are also more filling. I always make extra filling to have leftovers.

8 1-inch-thick slices of crusty sourdough bread, grilled or oven-toasted on both sides
1 pound lobster meat, steamed and sliced *
½ cup chopped fresh chives
½ cup chopped flat-leaf fresh parsley
3 hot serrano chilies, chopped
½ cup mayonnaise
2 tablespoons very good, unfiltered extra virgin olive oil
1 teaspoon freshly crushed black pepper
salt
1 cup finely diced celery

**1** Place the bread slices on a platter.

**2** Combine the remaining ingredients in a bowl; mix well.

**3** Top each slice of bread with approximately 2 to 3 heaping tablespoons of the lobster mixture. Serve as an appetizer. If making these for a cocktail party, cut each slice of bread into smaller, bite-size pieces, and top with just a teaspoon of the lobster mixture. SERVES 6–8

**NOTE** For a variation or when lobster isn't available, try substituting a firm white fish, poached; cooked shrimp and crab are also lovely.

# Jhoti, the Peanut Man

I grew up on Elliott's Beach in Madras (Chennai), on the eastern coast of India. Every evening, my cousins and I would skip alongside my grandfather as he brandished his carved walking stick down the stairs from our flat, across Second Avenue, and down Beach Road while he waved to all the neighbors along the way. The path was covered in sand, and we would all walk barefoot to the shore where the whole of our village, Besant Nagar, came to socialize.

From our veranda you could see the Indian Ocean and the sun rising above it every morning. Because of the heat, the beach was off-limits to us until the end of the day, and because of the waves, we could be there only with an elder member of our family. On Elliott's Beach one could see people sitting in circles playing cards, young lovers trying to meet furtively, gangs of teenagers whooping and chiding each other, and what seemed like millions of children playing like crabs on the sand. In those days, there were still shells to collect, and we always competed to gather the best loot. Points were given for size and how perfectly intact a shell was, but we also acknowledged the superior beauty of a particular shell. We were allowed to get our feet wet, but my grandparents loathed getting wet themselves, and often we were discouraged from going further into the water lest they had to rescue us.

Once in a while you saw a lady who dared to go into the water. Because she didn't want to hitch up her sari and bare her legs, the sari would balloon out around her as she submerged herself with squeals of terror and pleasure. Most Indians at that time could hardly swim.

The best moment of the evening came when I heard the distant cry of Jhoti, the peanut man. He always wore a wrinkled plaid cotton dhoti, which he folded upward to expose his leathery black legs. He balanced a wicker basket on his head with one arm. A rectangular tin box swung from a semicircular handle in the other. Once we heard his cry, we dropped all other pursuits. No matter what we were doing, building sand castles, trading shells, or playing the most violent game of tag, we always, always came to a frozen halt when we heard Jhoti's cry. My grandfather would be sitting nearby with a cluster of retired judges, discussing some pressing political issue of the day, and we would descend on him, pleading like little birds for rupees to buy those delicious morsels we knew lay deep within the basket on top of Jhoti's head. My grandfather always kept a few rupee coins tied inside a knot at the waist of his white veshti (the brahmin dhoti), and we beseeched him to perform the embarrassing task of untying the money at his waist in front of the most venerable seniors of the neighborhood. If instead he reached inside the breast pocket of his bush shirt for paper money, we knew that there was a particularly distinguished colleague or stranger in the group, in front of whom he did not feel comfortable untying the knot. At times, he shooed us away, and we'd be forced to go to my grandmother, who never carried much money in the evenings.

Jhoti's basket and tin box had every savory snack one could imagine. In his basket, he had salted plantain chips, puffed rice mixed with fried semolina and curry leaves, and peanuts that were dry-roasted with salt, chili powder, or lemon and black cumin salt. He had peanuts covered in batter, roasted with molasses. He had diced tomatoes with fresh coriander, green chilies, and salt to mix with the treasure I coveted most: boiled peanuts, which were secure from the elements in the tin box. I loved those steaming hot, boiled peanuts. Jhoti would put a shell scoop full of boiled peanuts in a bowl made of dry lotus leaves. He then folded in the tomato concoction and finished it off with a squeeze of lime juice. The peanuts had a soft and tangy taste, and when quickly mixed by Jhoti's deft hand, all the flavors, and the simultaneous sensations of hot and cold, would burst with every mouthful. You'd taste the freshness of the coriander, the spiky bite of the green chilies, and the sourness of the lemon. All this was anchored by the buttery, warm taste of crumbling peanuts. These peanuts were wet and moist, not dry and coarse—more of a delicacy than a snack.

In those days I had little desire for anything other than my mini nut salad in a dried leaf bowl. My nose became so trained by my desire for what lay at the bottom of Jhoti's tin box that I often began to sense the smell of those peanuts before I heard his cries from down the shore. They smelled like boiling rice but without its starchy velvet scent. I later recognized that smell from my childhood memories as having a distinct aroma of bay leaf. Jhoti would often throw a bay leaf into the water, I am sure of it.

Eventually Jhoti earned enough to buy a cart with a bell that he would pull as he entered a lane in our neighborhood. He would pull his string to produce a metal tap and then there would be a ding half a beat later. We began to listen for that sound. He had also invested in a balancing scale; he would measure out his peanuts on one side while piling octagonal iron weights into the other. By the time I was in fourth grade he favored cones of newspaper instead of the dried lotus leaf bowls his mother had patiently stitched for him. I hated the newspaper cones as they always became soggy with the lime and tomato juices seeping into them. I lamented aloud to him that I missed the days when he used to trawl the beach with his basket and box, and complained about the missing bowls. He said his mother was growing old and could not keep up the pace of bowl production needed for his expanded business. Plus he spoke of soreness in his arms and shoulders. "What do you care?" he quipped. "You're in America now. You only come here on holidays." "Yes, but I dream of these peanuts the whole way on the plane!" I retorted. "Then bring your bowl down from upstairs. I'll fill that." It was an acceptable compromise, but nothing would ever taste as lovely as those peanuts mixed with a few flying grains of sand that I ate off lotus leaves when I was six. He said the sea air also made them taste good and often teasingly suggested I take my metal bowl to the shore and eat my peanuts on the sand. I once brought him a t-shirt from the United States, but I never saw him wear it. He said he was saving it for a special occasion.

When I was in high school, Jhoti's cousin took over the peanut cart. He stopped carrying the boiled peanuts altogether, and now the recipe survives only among those of us who remember those evenings on the beach in the late seventies when Second Avenue was still covered in sand, and there were still shells on the shore.

# WARM PEANUT SALAD

1 medium-size bay leaf, fresh or dried
1 pound raw peanuts, shelled (1 ¾ pounds in
   the shell)
½ pound tomatoes
1 cup chopped fresh cilantro
2 green Thai chilies, finely minced (or less,
   to taste)
1 tablespoon sea salt
   juice of 2 very ripe lemons or ¼ cup juice

**1** In a large pot, bring 5 cups of water to a boil. Add the bay leaf. Keep the water at a rolling boil, add all the peanuts and cook for about 30 minutes or until a peanut crumbles easily under the pressure of a fork's tine.

**2** While the peanuts are boiling, remove the seeds from the tomatoes and dice them finely with a sharp knife.

**3** Combine the cilantro with the tomato, and add the green chilies.

**4** Drain the boiled peanuts very well, and remove the bay leaf.

**5** Toss the peanuts with the tomato mixture. Add salt and lemon juice. Stir well and serve immediately. SERVES 6–8

# DEVILED EGGS WITH SERRANO CHILIES

My sweet friend Antonia once said that while her husband Harold can seem very complicated, all he really needs to keep him happy is a boiled egg or two in the morning. I do think that eggs are something so basic, that we often overlook them. I started making these very retro appetizers for cocktail parties because many of my guests were on high protein, low starch diets. I love these deviled eggs because they're so easy and well, we all have eggs in the fridge. So they're great to whip up at the last minute or to help stretch the food if you have unexpected crashers. The green chilies and coriander give them a fresh spiky taste, and make them slightly more piquant than traditional ones.

⅓ cup mayonnaise
1 serrano chili, seeded and minced
3 grape tomatoes, seeded and diced finely with
    skin
2 tablespoons minced fresh cilantro
1 tablespoon balsamic vinegar
    salt
    a squirt of fresh lemon juice, about a teaspoon
6 hard-boiled eggs

**1** Combine all the ingredients, except the eggs, in a bowl. Set aside.

**2** Carefully peel the eggs, without scratching the whites. Slice each egg lengthwise and toss the yolks into the bowl with all the other ingredients. Arrange the whites on a platter.

**3** Mix the contents of the bowl well by mashing them together with a fork; add salt to taste. Using a spoon, put a bit of the yolk mixture back into each of the whites and serve them on a platter at room temperature. SERVES 4–6

## HOW TO BOIL AND PEEL EGGS

Making perfect boiled eggs is pretty simple. Just place the eggs in a deep saucepan, and make sure to cover them with enough cold water so that there is at least an inch of water above the eggs. Now pour 2 tablespoons of salt over the eggs. Place the pan on high heat. Once the water is boiling continue to cook the eggs for 4 minutes. While the eggs are boiling, prepare a large bowl of ice and water in the sink ready for immersing the eggs. Drain boiled eggs in a colander and then put them immediately into the ice bath. Leave them there for 20 minutes. When peeling, break the shell on the kitchen counter and roll them so tiny cracks are formed all around the shell. This should make it easier to peel. Start at the widest end of the egg and strip peel in a circular motion around the egg as much as possible. Rinse the egg to free any tiny pieces of shell. Wipe egg off with a paper towel. Easy boiled eggs.

# SPICED CANDIED PECANS

These nuts are a sweet and savory snack that can be made hot on the spot with just a few minutes in the oven. They tend not to last very long, so while I have given the recipe for just 2 servings, you may find yourself doubling it automatically after the first time. If you're in a rush, they can be made even more quickly on the stove in a non-stick frying pan by drizzling the maple syrup and chili over the nuts and stirring constantly on medium heat with a wooden spoon to avoid burning. That way is a bit trickier, so I give the baked version of the recipe below. The pecans will keep in plastic bags, once cooled, for up to 2 weeks, and are great sprinkled on top of spinach or arugula salads as well. Always keep pecans on hand for an impromptu batch of these beauties. One cup of nuts should last long enough for two people to enjoy a cold beer.

1 cup whole pecans
¼ cup maple syrup
¼ teaspoon chili powder

**1** Preheat the oven to 375°F. Line a baking sheet with aluminum foil.

**2** Arrange the pecans on the baking sheet in a single layer. Try to keep the individual nuts from touching each other.

**3** In a small bowl, whisk the maple syrup and chili powder together with a fork. Now drizzle the syrup over the pecans. Try to coat the nuts completely by sliding them around on the baking sheet so all the syrup is used. Place in the oven and bake for 10 to 12 minutes, until the syrup has just begun to brown or blacken; don't let the nuts burn.

**4** Remove and immediately arrange the pecans on a dish, making sure they do not touch one another; if you leave them in a pile, they will cool into a brittle. SERVES 2

# ROOT VEGETABLE CARPACCIO

This light and refreshing dish is best served in high summer as a first course with some freshly baked bread or focaccia. It can be made hours ahead and kept crisp in the fridge until just before serving. I would wait until then to drizzle the dressing, as the vegetable slices can get soggy if they sit too long in liquid.

10 red radishes, trimmed, scrubbed, and thinly sliced
1 large jicama, peeled and thinly sliced *
2 tablespoons minced fresh hot red pepper
2 to 3 tablespoons extra virgin olive oil (unfiltered if possible)
    juice of 1 ripe lemon
    coarsely ground sea salt (preferably fleur de sel)

**1** Spread the radish and jicama slices, alternately and one layer thick, on a large platter.

**2** In a bowl, mix the minced pepper with the olive oil and lemon juice.

**3** Drizzle the dressing over the vegetables and sprinkle with salt. SERVES 4–6

**NOTE** If you can't find jicama, substitute white radish. This dish then becomes a lovely red and white radish carpaccio.

# POCHETTES OF FETA, TOMATO, AND BASIL

I know this recipe seems a bit labor-intensive, but it is well worth it when you want to impress your dinner guests with something spectacular. It is a definite crowd pleaser. The thing to remember is not to let working with the filo pastry intimidate you. Just stay calm and give yourself lots of time for the project. I assemble the pochettes a couple of hours ahead and pop them in the oven just 10 minutes before guests arrive, keeping them warm in the turned-off oven if necessary.

1 1-pound package filo dough (about 30 sheets
   measuring 17 inches by 12 inches)
5 plum tomatoes
10 ounces Greek feta cheese, crumbled
2 cups loosely packed, finely chopped fresh basil
½ teaspoon crushed dried red pepper
   salt (optional)
1 cup (2 sticks) butter, clarified

**1** Remove the filo from the refrigerator 30 minutes before starting.

**2** Slice the tomatoes lengthwise and scoop out the seeds with a spoon. Squeeze gently to eliminate excess liquid. It's important to get the tomatoes as dry as possible. Wipe dry, inside and out, with a paper towel. When the tomatoes are dry, dice them.

**3** In a bowl, combine the tomatoes, feta, basil, and crushed red pepper to form a salad. Add a pinch of salt only if needed.

**4** Prepare the filo dough by laying out a clean dishcloth on a flat surface. Make sure both surface and cloth are large enough to accommodate the flat filo. Stack the filo on the cloth, and cover with another dishcloth. With hot water, dampen and wring out a third cloth and lay that flat over the top cloth.

**5** Preheat the oven to 375°F.

**6** Cut the filo stack carefully—with kitchen scissors, as knives tend to tear the pastry—into 8-inch squares. Remove 3 squares of the filo at a time, keeping the rest under the towels.

**7** Take 1 sheet and brush it with the clarified butter. Place a second sheet of the filo at a 45° angle over the first, and brush this with butter as well. Place the third sheet of filo at a 45° angle over the second, and brush this with the clarified butter.

**8** Now spoon 1 to 2 tablespoons of the tomato salad onto the center of the filo. Gather together the corners of the filo and twist the packet ends gently, as you would the ends of a hard-candy wrapper. Fan out the ends into a rose floret. Then peel down the petals to fan out a nice crown. Brush the top of the pochette with more clarified butter. Repeat this process until you have about 10.

**9** Place the pochettes on a baking sheet in the preheated oven for 10 to 12 minutes, until the sides are golden brown. Serve warm. SERVES 6–8

# GRILLED MANCHEGO BITES WITH APRICOT PRESERVES

A few years ago, I started seeing what looked like bite-size grilled cheese sandwiches being passed around at parties that were very fashionably catered. It occurred to me that if these high-end types could steal such a homemade specialty and turn it into party food, then I could steal it back for parties at home. The following recipe is my version of mini grilled cheese appetizers. They can also be left uncut and served, with a small salad, as a great lunch for one. For this recipe, it is important to find soft manchego cheese because the harder cheeses will not melt as easily. Make sure to ask your cheese seller to show you the various types of manchego, or at least make sure you buy from a shop that has a high turnover, as cheese tends to get harder as it ages. There are different types of manchego, the artisenal kind tends to be younger and softer. The quality of the cheese turns this from being a simple grilled cheese sandwich into an appetizer that's easy to make but tastes quite complicated and interesting. The apricot preserves and fresh herbs elevate this dish into bite-size pillows of melted heaven. The recipe serves 4, but it's easy to multiply if you're making these to pass around for a party.

4 slices sourdough bread
 apricot preserves
3 or 4 ¼-inch-thick slices Spanish manchego
 artesano cheese (approximately 2 to 3 ounces)
3-inch sprig fresh thyme, which yields
 about ½ teaspoon of leaves
 butter at room temperature

**1** Take 2 of the 4 slices of bread. Thinly spread the apricot preserves on one side of each slice as you would on breakfast toast. On the other 2 slices, position the cheese so that the entire surface is covered (it's okay to break up the cheese in order to cover the entire area).

**2** Strip a sprig of thyme and sprinkle the herb over the cheese. Fresh thyme is quite strong, so you don't have to use every last leaf. Place the apricot-spread slices of bread over the cheese, and generously butter the outsides of each sandwich.

**3** Heat both sandwiches in a pan over low heat and cover the pan. Cook for 5 to 6 minutes (until the pan side of the bread is nicely browned). Now carefully turn over each sandwich with a spatula and cover the pan again. After 2 to 3 minutes, when you can see the cheese melting on the sides, remove the lid to let out the steam so the sandwich does not get soggy. Cook just until both sides are golden brown. Now place the sandwiches on a plate and, with a sharp serrated knife, carefully cut them into bite-size squares. Serve while still hot. SERVES 4

# SALADS

# BASIL AND BLOOD ORANGE SALAD

I first tasted a version of this salad on a farm at the base of the Alpujarra mountains in Spain, while filming my documentary *Planet Food* for the Food Network. A sweet woman named Mercedes cooked all day long while her husband, Paco, tended the animals. The salad is not only glorious to eat but beautiful to look at. The glistening oranges, jeweled with dried cranberries, sit regally in a luxurious bed of dark green spinach that's laced with the spiky fragrance of basil. The nuttiness of the pepitas completes the odyssey of taste and texture. It never fails to be a hit.

**DRESSING**
¼ cup olive oil
2 tablespoons balsamic vinegar
1 tablespoon yuzu or lime juice
1 teaspoon crushed Sichuan peppercorns *
   coarsely ground rock salt

**SALAD**
4 blood oranges, peeled, seeded, pith removed,
   and sliced into semicircles **
1 small red onion sliced into thin rings
5 ounces spinach leaves
3 cups fresh basil leaves, stems removed
1 cup dried cranberries
1 cup pepitas (pumpkin seeds), roasted and salted

**1** Mix all the dressing ingredients in a large bowl.

**2** Toss the oranges, onions, and cranberries in the dressing, and stir to coat well.

**3** In a large salad bowl, mix together the basil and spinach. Just before serving, toss in the orange and onion mixture, and mix well (adding the onion mixture too soon will make the salad soggy). Sprinkle pepitas on top and serve immediately. SERVES 4–6

**NOTE** You can use regular peppercorns as well, but Sichuan ones have a smoky flavor that gives a distinct aroma to dishes.

You can also make this recipe with navel oranges if blood oranges are not easily available.

## ASIAN COLE SLAW WITH LIMA BEANS AND RED CABBAGE

I first had a version of this salad down the street from my apartment in West Hollywood at the King's Road café. It's a hangout for young Hollywood types who need to watch their figures—this salad is an antidote to the creamy, rich coleslaw that's usually served at diners. It's great paired with a sandwich for lunch or next to a nice piece of simple grilled fish. I make mine with lima beans to give it a charming retro feel. The magenta shreds of cabbage add a robust color to any buffet or sit-down meal.

1 cup frozen lima beans
5 cups red cabbage, chopped in shreds
½ teaspoon salt
2 green chilies, minced or chopped
1 cup chopped cilantro leaves
2 carrots, grated
3 tablespoons lemon juice
3 tablespoons toasted sesame oil
1 tablespoon sherry or wine vinegar

**1** Boil the lima beans until tender, about 10 minutes. Drain and dry them with paper towels.

**2** Chop the cabbage into small shreds (like coleslaw). Add the salt, chilies, cilantro, carrots, and lima beans. Mix all these together well in a large bowl.

**3** In a small bowl, whisk together the lemon juice, sesame oil, and vinegar.

**4** Pour the dressing over the cabbage and stir well to distribute the dressing evenly.

**5** This dish can be made hours ahead of serving as the cabbage actually soaks in the dressing flavors better if left to sit for at least an hour or two beforehand. SERVES 4–6

## ZA'ATAR POWDER: ENDLESS POSSIBILITIES

Za'atar powder is a Middle Eastern spice powder that is mainly used in Syria and parts of Armenia and Turkey. It contains oregano, thyme, and sesame seeds as well as sumac. It's an excellent seasoning to rub on freshly baked breads—especially flatbreads, as they do in the Middle East. Like sumac, za'atar powder will keep for ages in your pantry. I always keep it in mine to help me literally make something out of almost nothing. You can make a lovely yogurt dip for crudités and flatbreads or chips by simply mixing za'atar and some fresh herbs into the yogurt. Use 2 teaspoons of za'atar for every cup of plain yogurt or sour cream, and add whatever tender fresh herbs you have in the fridge. Chives, cilantro, and especially mint go splendidly well with this dip, but dill and even tarragon are fine. Add 2 tablespoons of chopped fresh mint or cilantro, and just 1 tablespoon of chives, as they are more strongly flavored. Adjust the salt, if needed, and garnish with a sprinkle of sumac. You can also add za'atar to sandwiches and roasts, as well as garnish potato salads with it. The possibilities are endless.

# CARROT AND CILANTRO SALAD

I grew up in India eating small diced or grated salads called kachumbers. They provided a fresh respite from many of the spicy lentil dishes and curries that were often served at the family table. I like biting into cool, crunchy fresh vegetables in the middle of a hot meal. In the Middle East, small chopped salads are served as part of the mezze, or first course. In Spain many tapas dishes are also small servings of marinated vegetables. This salad goes well with roasts, poultry, and seafood, and is good summer or winter. The addition of pure orange oil gives the salad a luxurious taste and the aroma of a thousand tangerines.

**DRESSING**
¼ cup olive oil
4 tablespoons balsamic vinegar
2 tablespoons fresh lime juice
¼ teaspoon pure orange oil

**SALAD**
2 pounds carrots, shredded
2 ½ cups cilantro leaves
¼ cup white hulled sesame seeds, dry-roasted
   in a frying pan until golden brown on medium
   heat (approximately 5 to 6 minutes)
4 hot green chilies, minced
⅓ cup dried cranberries
¼ teaspoon za'atar powder
½ teaspoon fleur de sel or other good sea salt

**1** Combine all the ingredients for the salad dressing together in the bottom of a salad bowl.

**2** In the same bowl, toss together all the other ingredients except the za'atar powder and the salt. Sprinkle the za'atar powder and salt on top of the salad just before serving. SERVES 4–6

## TANGY JICAMA SALAD

I like to call this my "shoestring salad," because of all the thinly chopped vegetables. I suggest you undertake the chopping while watching a recorded episode or two of your favorite show. Just remember to watch your fingers while wielding the knife! The layered textures, as you crunch into the salad, make it worth the labor. There are many inexpensive Japanese slicers that are easy to use and have a setting that will achieve the desired effect. But at the end of the day, it's just one apple and one jicama, so you might as well use a good knife. The jicama gives this salad a strange scratchy feel on the tongue that's nicely offset by the smooth texture of the sweet, tart crisp apple. I leave the apple unpeeled, not only for added color but for texture. Perfect for picnics and barbeques, this salad is a refreshing accompaniment to anything from grilled fish and meat to roast chicken to hamburgers and kabobs.

1 large jicama, peeled and cut into shoestrings
1 Granny Smith apple, cored and cut into
    shoestrings
1 serrano green chili, minced with seeds
1 red bell pepper, diced
1 cup chopped fresh cilantro
    juice of 1 very ripe lemon
2 tablespoons fresh chopped chives
    salt

**1** Mix all the ingredients in a bowl and toss well together. Serve right away or chill in the refrigerator for up to 2 days. SERVES 4–6

# A VERY HERBACEOUS SALAD

I had a similar salad once at my Iranian friend Nasi's house. She is an amazing cook and often thinks nothing of cooking for 50 people with no help at all. I don't know how she does it, but she does, every year when her husband, Peter throws a lavish dinner party for filmmakers in their home. I always beg her for a doggy bag and live with pleasure on her leftovers for days.

**DRESSING**
2 tablespoons light mayonnaise
1 tablespoon sherry vinegar
1 teaspoon freshly ground black pepper
⅛ teaspoon coarse sea salt

**SALAD**
1 English cucumber, peeled and cut into disks
1 large head romaine lettuce, cut in large sections
⅓ cup chopped flat-leaf parsley
⅓ cup chopped fresh dill
⅓ cup chopped mint

**1** Whisk all of the dressing ingredients together vigorously in the bottom of a large salad bowl. Refrigerate if you're not serving immediately.

**2** Just before serving, toss the cucumber and all of the greens into the bowl, and mix well to make sure the dressing is evenly distributed. Serve immediately. **SERVES 4–6**

# PONDICHERRY LENTIL SALAD

I named this salad after a town in South India that was heavily influenced by French colonization. I love the easy mix of Eastern and Western flavors that this recipe exemplifies. The salad is made with small black lentils similar to French puy lentils but can be made with any black lentils. Here I use lentils that are named beluga, after the caviar, because of their appearance and minuscule size, especially when compared to other lentils. I love the crispness of the apple and peppers mingling with the soft texture of the lentils. This is a great salad to take on a picnic, and especially handy if you're serving vegetarians who need a bit of substance to their meal. The ginger and coconut roasted in sesame oil give it a richer flavor than most run-of-the-mill lentil salads.

2 cups beluga black lentils
1 Fuji apple, cored and diced
1 yellow bell pepper, diced
1 large jalapeño pepper, diced
⅛ cup olive oil
1 tablespoon balsamic vinegar
  juice of 1 ½ ripe lemons
1 teaspoon salt
1 cup loosely packed, chopped flat-leaf parsley
1 tablespoon sesame oil
1 ½ tablespoons minced fresh ginger
¼ cup shredded unsweetened coconut

**1** Wash the lentils and soak them for 2 hours in tepid water; drain.

**2** In a deep pot, add 8 cups of water to the lentils, bring to a boil, cover, and cook on low heat for 20 to 25 minutes. Rinse the lentils with cold water and drain. Make sure the lentils are cooked but firm, not mushy.

**3** In a large bowl, mix together the lentils, apple, bell pepper, jalapeño, olive oil, vinegar, lemon juice, salt, and parsley. Stir and set aside in the fridge.

**4** Just before serving, heat the sesame oil on medium-high heat. When hot, roast the ginger and coconut for a few minutes until golden and toasty. Sprinkle this garnish over the lentils and serve immediately. SERVES 6

# SPINACH AND BLACK PLUM SALAD

This salad is simple yet has a bold and beguiling taste. I first started to use mint in my salads because it had literally taken over the front yard of my mother's house, providing a green velvet sea that enveloped the stems of her rose bushes. After the chutneys and jams, the mint made its way into almost every dish for a while. It elevates the spinach leaves with a cool aftertaste, and the black plums give the salad a burst of fleshy, sweet tartness. We had an abundance of those as well, as our neighbor Margaret had a tree that rained them down on us all season long.

**DRESSING**
5 tablespoons olive oil
1 tablespoon balsamic vinegar
1 tablespoon yuzu juice (see page 14)
    juice of 1 ripe lemon
    freshly ground black pepper

**SALAD**
3 black plums, firm and not too ripe, pitted
    and sliced
½ cup torn fresh mint leaves
6 ounces baby spinach leaves
    crushed sea salt

**1** Combine the dressing ingredients in the bottom of a salad bowl.

**2** Just before serving, add the salad ingredients, except the salt, and toss.

**3** Now sprinkle the sea salt over this. (I prefer to add the sea salt last so you get grainy bits of it intact rather than have it dissolve into the dressing.) SERVES 6

ゆずの㊜しぼり汁

香りの宝石・種まき

ゆず
粋の

東佐登録 419666番

高知県安芸市尾川甲216
小　松　燗

## FENNEL AND HERB SALAD WITH LABNEH CHEESE

I can't remember how I invented this salad, but I think I came home one day with a bottle of fantastic Labneh goat cheese steeped in olive oil and herbs. I'd never seen it that way before, but it's actually a great way to store goat cheese as it keeps forever in the fridge. All you need are some fresh herbs and fennel to make a lush first course or a great side dish to any meal. I love the way the crisp fennel pierces the creaminess of the goat cheese. If you can't find the cheese steeped in oil (though it's available in most Middle Eastern or gourmet stores) just use regular Labneh or another fresh goat cheese. Form it into knobs, and pour some olive oil into a dish and turn the knobs around in it (this keeps them from sticking or getting gooey). Then dot the salad with the cheese.

2 large fennel bulbs, green tops removed, sliced
   in very thin vertical pieces
⅓ cup chopped flat-leaf parsley
¼ cup chopped fresh dill
1 tablespoon chopped fresh tarragon leaves
2 to 3 tablespoons extra virgin olive oil,
   unfiltered, if possible
   juice of 1 ripe lemon
10 to12 balls Labneh goat cheese in oil

**1** Toss all ingredients except the cheese together in a bowl or on a flat platter.

**2** Dot with the cheese and serve. SERVES 4–6

# TUNA AND RED BEAN SALAD

This is one of those versatile salads that makes a great lunch for 4, served with just some fresh baked bread, or a nice, light starter for 6 people. It's great for summer because the only cooking involves lighting the grill. It's also healthy enough to help you prepare for bathing suit season.

**DRESSING**
juice of 1 very ripe lemon
¼ cup olive oil
2 teaspoons balsamic vinegar
½ teaspoon dried oregano
    salt

**SALAD**
12-ounce tuna steak, about 1 inch thick
5 ounces mixed baby lettuces and field greens
10 ounces fresh or frozen artichoke bottoms,
    blanched if frozen; scraped and cored,
    steamed, and quartered if fresh
1 cup sliced English cucumber
1 cup halved cherry or grape tomatoes
½ cup fresh-snipped chives
½ cup chopped fresh flat-leaf parsley
1 10-ounce can red kidney beans, drained and
    rinsed

**1** Light the grill so that the coals get nice and hot. When the flames have died down and the coals are glowing red and white, sear the tuna on the grill for about 3 minutes on each side; the exact time will depend on the tuna's thickness and how rare you want it.

**2** Mix all the dressing ingredients in a small bowl or screw-top jar.

**3** Lay a bed of lettuce and field greens in a large salad bowl or platter.

**4** In a separate bowl toss together the artichokes, cucumber, tomatoes, chives, parsley, and drained kidney beans.

5. Spoon this vegetable mixture in a mound in the center of the greens.

**6** Slice the tuna steak into ¼-inch slices. Lay the slices decoratively over the mound of vegetables.

**7** Just before serving, drizzle the dressing evenly over the salad. SERVES 4–6

# BLACK GRAPES AND BABY ARUGULA

This is a very elegant salad that looks much fancier than its parts. I sometimes substitute grape-seed oil for the olive oil; both work beautifully. The dressing has a hidden fragrance of citrus that is at once mysterious and delicious. It's not a bad idea to keep extra batches of the dressing on hand to use on other salads. When people ask you what that hidden flavor is, look heavenward and say, "Oh … just a bit of magic."

## DRESSING
2 ½ tablespoons extra virgin olive oil or
   grape-seed oil
¾ tablespoons balsamic vinegar, the more aged
   the better
¼ teaspoon freshly ground black peppercorns
   a few drops orange oil (optional but strongly
   recommended)

## SALAD
2 dozen seedless black grapes, halved vertically
7 cups baby arugula
2 ripe, firm Bartlett pears, sliced lengthwise,
   cored and peeled
2 cups loosely packed, stemmed, ripped fresh
   cilantro
1 teaspoon fleur de sel or other sea salt
4 ounces fresh sheep's milk cheese (such as
   pecorino), sliced as thinly as possible.

**1** In a small bowl, whisk together the ingredients for the dressing. Set aside.

**2** In a large platter or salad bowl, toss together the grapes, arugula, pear slices, and cilantro.

**3** Now pour the dressing over the salad and toss again.

**4** Grind the sea salt over the salad.

**5** Lay the slices of cheese over the salad and serve immediately. SERVES 6

# SOUPS

# PERSIAN CHICKEN SOUP WITH OMANI LEMON AND DILL

I first discovered Omani lemons in London. They are jewels of flavor that last in your cupboard for ages—even for a whole year. These dried citrus fruits come from Iran and are used in soups and stews as souring agents. They come in white and black, and the two work equally well. With a wonderful, musky quality that is very hard to describe and that is not unlike the aroma dried mushrooms or truffles impart to a dish, they provide acidity, too. I use them in soups but also in roasts and sauces, and even with braised meats and vegetables. Because of their acidity, they are best used in tomato-based rather than cream-based dishes. They are quite strong in flavor, so I recommend crushing them with a mallot (they will shatter easily into many bits) and experimenting with them in small doses.

2 carrots, scraped, cut on the diagonal in ½-inch
   chunks
1 large sweet onion, peeled and quartered
3 cloves garlic, peeled
1 teaspoon black peppercorns
10 juniper berries
1 Persian Omani dried lemon, crushed with a mallot
3 chicken thighs, on the bone
2 cups loosely packed snipped fresh dill
2 heaping tablespoons salt
2 tablespoons olive oil
2 shallots, diced
3 plum tomatoes
1 ½ cups drained, canned chick-peas

**1** Mix together the carrots, sweet onion, garlic, peppercorns, juniper berries, dried Omani lemon, chicken, 1 cup of the dill, 2 quarts of water, and salt in a deep pot. Cover and cook over medium heat for 1 hour, stirring occasionally.

**2** Remove the carrots and the chicken, placing the chicken on a dish and the carrots in a bowl. Let the chicken cool.

**3** Carefully strain the soup into a large bowl through a fine-mesh sieve, saving the ingredients but throwing out any fatty bits from the chicken.

**4** Puree the ingredients in the sieve and return them to the soup. When the chicken has cooled, tear the meat from the bones, and chop it into small pieces, again discarding fatty bits.

**5** In another deep pot, heat the olive oil on medium heat, and stir-fry the shallots. When the shallots have softened, about 2 minutes, add the plum tomatoes. When the tomatoes have begun to peel and wrinkle (about 3 minutes more), add the stock to deglaze the pan. Replace the chicken and carrots. After stirring for a few minutes, add the chick-peas and the remaining 1 cup of fresh dill. Let the soup boil gently over medium-low heat for 5 to 10 minutes. Serve hot on a cold winter's day. SERVES 4–6

# HOT AND SOUR TOMATO BROTH WITH SHRIMP

When I was a child and in bed suffering from a cold or flu, the women in my house always made a traditional South Indian soup called rasam. There are many variations, some with lemon, others with cumin, some with lentils or garlic or a mix of these. I always loved this soup but thought it lacked a bit of substance for the Western palate, and so I've made this version with shrimp. It still remains quite a light soup, and it's sure to cure you of all your ailments. I sometimes add some rice noodles when I'm feeling too sick to cook a whole meal. The fragrant blend of cilantro, cumin, and tamarind clears the head and washes away the aches and pains we suffer during flu season. It's light enough to serve in the spring and summer, too. It's also very low calorie, as well as low in carbs and high in protein for those of us watching our waistlines. There are several ingredients—fenugreek seeds, asafetida powder, jaggery, and black mustard seeds—that you may not have in your pantry. All these can be bought at an Indian or Asian grocery for less than $15. The taste of this broth is well worth the effort to get these items. They will keep in your cupboard for months, and you'll be well stocked for many other recipes too.

2 1-ounce knobs (2 golf-ball size pieces) of
    tamarind pulp (see page 66)
12 ounces peeled, deveined shrimp
    juice of 1 ripe lemon
    salt
1 ½ tablespoons vegetable oil
¾ teaspoon black mustard seeds
¼ teaspoon fenugreek seeds
½ teaspoon cumin seeds
20 fresh curry leaves
3 cloves sliced garlic
½ teaspoon asafetida powder
2 cups halved grape or cherry tomatoes
1 to 2 fresh minced green chilies
½ teaspoon sambar curry powder (or Madras
    curry powder)
½-inch piece of jaggery (brown cane sugar or
    palm sugar)
1 tablespoon Thai fish sauce
¼ cup chopped fresh cilantro

**1** Soak the tamarind pulp in 6 cups of very hot water (bring it to a boil and then pour it over the tamarind) for 20 minutes and crush it with the back of a spoon to make a pulp.

**2** Marinate the shrimp in lemon juice and a pinch of salt. Set aside in the fridge.

**3** In a deep soup pot, heat the vegetable oil on medium heat and add the mustard seeds, fenugreek, cumin seeds, curry leaves, and garlic, and cook for 3 to 4 minutes. As soon as the mustard seeds begin to pop and crackle out of the pan, add the asafetida, tomatoes, and green chilies. Stir for a couple of minutes and then add the curry powder. Be careful as the mustard seeds will pop out of the pan!

**4** After about 4 to 5 minutes, when the tomatoes have started to wilt and become soft, pour in the strained tamarind gravy.

**5** Stir in the jaggery piece and the fish sauce, and heat for about 10 minutes. Make sure the jaggery dissolves completely. Adjust salt, if needed. Once the oil begins to separate, and little pools of oil form on the surface, add the shrimp and cook until just opaque, 2 to 3 minutes. Do not overcook the shrimp!

**6** Remove from the heat and stir in the cilantro. Serve piping hot in bowls. SERVES 4–6

## MAKING TAMARIND GRAVY

Tamarind is a sticky, sweet and sour fruit that grows
on trees in long pods. It is an ingredient in Worcestershire
sauce and adobo sauce, as well as many barbeque
sauces, grows in Asia and in Central and South America,
and is prevalent in the cuisines of those regions. It is
usually sold in ethnic markets in many forms, but buy
the pure tamarind pulp in compressed bricks. I like
the Thai kind best; the Indian variety is often too dry. You
can make tamarind gravy thick or thin, depending on
the ratio of tamarind to hot water. To do this, soak a knob
of tamarind in water that has been brought to a boil.
I usually use 1-ounce (golf-ball size) of tamarind to
1 ½ to 2 cups water for a medium-strength gravy. For
chutneys and sauces (when I don't want a lot of liquid),
I use only 1 cup of water to the 1 ounce of tamarind.
Push down on the knob with the back of a spoon, and it
will begin to dissolve and separate in the water. It usually
takes 20 minutes or so to extract most of the flavor.
At this point the water should be tepid. With either your
fingers or a spoon, mash up and knead the tamarind
in the water. Then pour this mixture through a fine-mesh
sieve into another bowl or directly into whatever dish
you're preparing. Smash the tamarind pulp into the
sieve with the back of a spoon to get as much gravy as
possible. You can reuse the tamarind for a thinner gravy
by running more hot water over the leftover tamarind
in the sieve, or immerse the sieve into another bowl
of hot water and then lift the sieve after a few minutes.

# CHICKEN SOUP WITH CUMIN AND LEMONGRASS

This soup is especially nourishing on a cold or rainy night. I know there are a lot of ingredients, but basically you just sauté all the seasonings, and then throw in the whole chicken, cover with liquid, and simmer until the meat is practically falling off the bone. In fact, it has many of the ingredients used in Asian remedies to keep colds at bay and is a marriage between Thai and Indian flavors. The ginger is common in both cuisines. The cumin and cloves are Indian and often used in broths to stave off cold and flu symptoms. The lemongrass and lime leaf are Thai, and employed to do the same. Both can now be found fresh in many good food stores and are readily available in Asian markets. I tend to buy large amounts when I find them. I freeze them for multiple uses, although they will keep in your crisper for up to 10 days. Both add a lemony fragrance as well as a purifying element to the chicken stock. Lemongrass is also a major component of Tiger Balm ointment and is used to soothe away all kinds of aches and pains. (Tiger Balm is perhaps the best-known brand of an ointment that is used in many Asian cultures, including in Thai and Indian traditional medicine.)

3 tablespoons olive oil
½ teaspoon cumin seeds
1 onion, chopped
4 cloves garlic, crushed
2 stalks lemongrass, cut into 4- to 5-inch pieces
   and split down the middle
2 green chilies, sliced
2 tablespoons minced ginger
4 cloves
5 kaffir lime leaves *
2 carrots cut into ½-inch pieces
2 potatoes, peeled and cut into 16 pieces
1 small whole peeled onion
1 chicken (2 to 3 pounds)
2 cups chicken stock
4 large celery stalks, cut into 1-inch pieces
   salt

**1** In a large, deep pot heat 3 tablespoons of olive oil over medium heat. To the hot oil, add the cumin seeds; stir for 2 minutes. Add the chopped onion, garlic, lemongrass, green chilies, ginger, cloves, and lime leaves; stir for 4 minutes.

**2** Add the carrots and potatoes. Stir.

**3** Stuff the cavity of the chicken with the whole peeled onion and add to the pot. Turn the chicken over and over to coat well with the sautéed mixture. Pour the chicken stock over the chicken and add more warm water, just enough to cover the chicken. Simmer for 70 to 80 minutes.

**4** Remove the chicken, taking care to drain any of the broth in its cavity back into the pot so as to lose as little of the soup as possible. Cool the chicken on a cutting board. Discard the onion that was in the cavity.

**5** Reduce the heat to low and add the celery. While the celery is cooking, remove the chicken from the bones. Chop the cooked chicken meat into bite-size pieces and return it to the pot. Stir and cook until the celery is fully cooked but crisp and not falling apart; this should only be a few minutes after you've finished chopping and adding all of the chicken meat, at most.

**6** Add salt to taste if necessary.

**7** Remove the lemongrass and lime leaves before serving. SERVES 6–8

**NOTE** Kaffir lime leaves are found in Thai and Asian grocery stores.

# PASSATA OF WHITE BEANS AND SAGE

I love white beans. They are a great staple to keep in your pantry for stews and soups when you need something hearty but don't want a huge slab of meat. Plus, if you have vegetarians in your family, as I do, beans really come in handy. I make various versions of this soup. Sometimes I just serve it without pureeing it at the end, to leave it chunky (the non-pureed version is called a ribollita). The beans make the soup quite filling, but I sometimes throw a bit of leftover cooked rice in it and serve it as a complete meal in a bowl. I use canned beans but you can soak and boil your own dried ones too.

2 pounds white cannellini beans, canned
¼ cup olive oil
1 tablespoon butter
3 cups chopped shallots
2 carrots, cut into ½-inch pieces
2 bay leaves
¼ cup chopped fresh sage leaves
2 teaspoons dried thyme or ¾ teaspoon fresh
½ cup dry white wine
1 ½ cups chicken stock
¼ cup half-and-half or light cream
    crushed black peppercorns

**1** Drain the cannellini beans and set them aside.

**2** In a deep pot, heat the olive oil over medium heat. Add the butter and, being careful not to brown it (you may have to lower the heat once the butter is added), sauté the shallots, carrots, bay leaves, and sage. Once the shallots have softened and become glassy, about 3 to 5 minutes, add the thyme. After the thyme has softened, approximately 1 to 2 minutes, deglaze the pan with white wine and add the white beans. Stir for a few more minutes and add the chicken stock.

**3** Cook at a gentle boil for 10 minutes. Remove the pot from the heat, and carefully take out the bay leaves.

**4** Use an immersion blender to puree the soup until it has a smooth texture.

**5** Place the pot back on the heat and stir in the half-and-half or light cream, cooking on low heat for about 5 more minutes. Sprinkle crushed black peppercorns over the top just before serving. SERVES 6–8

# CREAMY BROCCOLI SOUP

This is without a doubt the richest soup in this book, because of the pine nuts. I wanted a nutty flavor to turn this into something special, something to distinguish it from all the cream of broccoli soups we've all tasted over the years. I suggest you serve the soup with a light second course to balance the meal. Or serve it with just a salad for a lunchtime feast.

3 tablespoons butter
3 cloves garlic, chopped
1 cup chopped shallots
1 teaspoon herbs de Provence
½ tablespoon pine nuts
1 pound broccoli, cut in chunks, with stems,
  tough ends discarded
2 ½ cups chicken stock
1 cup light cream or half-and-half
  salt
½ teaspoon freshly ground black pepper

**1** In a deep pan, melt the butter on medium-low heat and add the garlic. Cook for about 2 minutes or until garlic begins to turn golden, stirring occasionally. Add the shallots, stirring for a few more minutes until they become glassy and soften. Add the herbs and the pine nuts, stirring for a few more minutes, just until the pine nuts turn golden.

**2** Add the broccoli and stir for an additional 5 to 7 minutes, just until the broccoli begins to darken slightly in color and soften.

**3** Finally, add the chicken stock and simmer for 12 to 15 minutes, stirring intermittently until the broccoli is cooked through.

**4** Using an immersion blender, puree the soup until it's a smooth, uniform consistency.

**5** Replace on the heat, and slowly stir in the light cream. After a couple of minutes, once the cream has been mixed in well, add salt, if needed.

**6** Once the soup is heated through, add freshly ground black pepper and serve hot.
SERVES 4–6

# CHILLED CUCUMBER SOUP

Our friend Andrew, who is married to Camilla, came to our house one day with a roaring toothache, saying he would just watch us eat. This soup was one I whipped up in just a few minutes. It tastes of the cool, grassy notes of summer. Andrew managed to gulp down more than one bowl of the cool, creamy liquid without so much as a yelp of pain. It's also mild in flavor and spice, and perfect for finicky eaters who may grace your table.

1 English cucumber, peeled and cut into 8 pieces
2 cups nonfat yogurt
   small handful of mint leaves, stems removed,
   or 1 teaspoon dried mint
1 teaspoon coarse sea salt

**1** Combine the cucumber, yogurt, mint leaves, and salt in a blender, and blend until you get a smooth liquid. Chill and serve cold on a hot summer's day. SERVES 3–4

## YELLOW VELVET LENTIL SOUP WITH CUMIN AND DRIED PLUMS

I once went to the annual kite festival in Ahmedabad in Gujarat, in western India. It's a day of celebration when most people can be found on their roofs flying so many kites that the sky looks peppered with locusts. My host, the lovely and beautiful Kinnari, usually makes a feast for the 60 or so people who come through her home on that day. Gujarati food is known for its incredible variety of vegetables, lentils, and fruits. I love the lentil soups, or dals, the best. Gujarati dal has a slightly sweet and hot taste to it. This soup is inspired by the many luscious soups I tasted that weekend at Kinnari's house while flying colorful kites on the roof with the rest of the townsfolk.

3 cups orange (masoor) lentils, washed well with
    warm water and drained
1 bay leaf
1 teaspoon salt
2 tablespoons olive oil
1 teaspoon cumin seeds
½ cup chopped shallots
1 ½ tablespoons minced ginger
2 ½ tablespoons shredded unsweetened coconut
1 cup grape or cherry tomatoes, halved
    lengthwise
3 plum tomatoes, quartered
2 teaspoons curry powder
    juice of 1 lemon
10 dried plums, pitted, chopped to bits
1 cup freshly chopped cilantro leaves

**1** Fill a deep stew pot with the lentils, bay leaf, salt, and enough water to cover the ingredients by 1 inch. Simmer on very low heat for 1 hour.

**2** Heat the oil in a skillet and add the cumin seeds. After 2 minutes, add the shallots and ginger, and cook until shallots are glassy. Add the coconut and stir until the coconut is golden brown.

**3** Add all the tomatoes and the curry powder, and sauté on medium heat for about 5 minutes until the tomatoes start to wilt and lose their shape.

**4** When the mixture forms a cohesive paste, add it to the lentils, stirring over low heat until nicely combined. Remove the bay leaves.

**5** With an immersion blender, pulverize the lentils so that the whole mixture is roughly blended, but not totally liquefied.

**6** Remove the soup from the heat and add the lemon juice, chopped plums, and cilantro. Stir in these final ingredients and serve hot. SERVES 8

# A RUSTIC AND WILD MUSHROOM SOUP

When I was living in Italy, one of the great kitchen secrets I learned was to save the rinds of Parmesan cheese for soup. Most Italian cooks add an old Parmesan rind to give flavor to their minestrones and stews. What's even better is that the flavor it adds is unique—it cannot be duplicated any other way. I add it here to give body to this wonderful peasant soup of mushrooms, which is great served just with some fresh, hot, crusty bread and cheese as a lovely autumn lunch. You can add any variety of mushrooms you find at the produce market. It's the variety of the mushrooms that enhances the taste of this rustic soup. So from now on save your Parmesan cheese rinds.

4 tablespoons unsalted butter
2 tablespoons olive oil
4 cloves garlic, peeled and cut lengthwise
3 bay leaves
½ cup diced onion
½ pound white mushrooms, diced
½ pound portobello mushrooms, diced
½ pound shiitake mushrooms, diced
½ pound crimini mushrooms, diced
½ teaspoon crushed red pepper
1 teaspoon dried thyme
¾ ounce dried chanterelle mushrooms
6 cups chicken stock
1 large russet potato, peeled and diced,
    about 1 ½ cups
¼ cup snipped chives
    rind of Parmesan cheese (approximately
    2½  x 4 inches)
½ cup chopped flat-leaf parsley

**1** In a large pot over medium heat, heat the butter and oil. As the butter is melting, stir in the garlic and bay leaves. After 2 to 3 minutes, add the onions and sauté for a few minutes until the onions soften and become glassy. Add all the fresh mushrooms, along with the crushed red pepper and thyme. Cover the pot and let the mushrooms cook, stirring occasionally, for about 10 to 12 minutes.

**2** While the mushrooms are cooking, soak the dried chanterelle mushrooms for 10 minutes in very hot water that has come to the boil. Remove the mushrooms from the liquid, reserving the soaking water. Dice the chanterelles, and add them to the soup along with the soaking water.

**3** Add the chicken stock, potatoes, chives, and cheese rind. Allow the soup to cook for about 35 to 40 minutes more.

**4** When ready, remove the bay leaves and cheese rind. Stir in the parsley and adjust salt to taste. Serve hot. SERVES 6–8

# SOUTH INDIAN SPINACH AND LENTIL SOUP

1 cup orange (masoor) lentils
3 cups spinach, steamed, chopped, and drained
2 or 3 dried red chilies (3 inches long)
2 tablespoons yellow (urad) lentils
1 cup grated unsweetened coconut
1 tablespoon vegetable oil
1 teaspoon cumin seeds
1 tablespoon black mustard seeds
   salt

**1** Soak masoor lentils for 2 to 3 hours in tepid water. Drain and wash until water runs clear.

**2** Boil the lentils in 4 cups of water with a bit of salt until they are soft and mushy. You may need to add more water. That should take 30 to 40 minutes over medium heat, maintaining a constant rolling gentle boil. Make sure to skim away any foam off the top with a spoon.

**3** Once the lentils are soft, take a wooden spoon or mallet, and mash them until they form a gravy-like, thick liquid. It's fine if some lentils remain coarse.

**4** Squeeze excess moisture out of the spinach and add to the lentils. Mix well, adjusting salt to taste, if needed.

**5** In a wok or small frying pan, dry-roast the red dry chilies with the urad lentils. This should take just 4 minutes in a hot pan on medium heat. The lentils should be toasted golden brown.

**6** In a blender or processor, puree the roasted urads and chilies; add the coconut and make a smooth mixture. Add this to the masoor lentils and spinach, and continue boiling gently for a bit.

**7** Heat the oil in a frying pan on medium heat. When the oil is hot, add the cumin and mustard seeds. When the seeds start to crackle and pop out of the pan, turn off the heat, and pour the seeds and oil into the lentils. Stir and serve hot. SERVES 6–8

# CURRIED BUTTERNUT SQUASH SOUP

Last year we went on a safari in Tanzania to the plains of the Serengeti. The landscape was breathtaking, and the animals seemed out of this world. In fact, you felt like you were in their world. We camped not far from a watering hole in order to see as many animals as we could in the days we were there. To my surprise, what I also remember with much pleasure is the food. We had a great cook who prepared lavish meals night after night in the most meager kitchen facility. When the sun dipped down, the plains became quite cold, and our meals often started with a soup. I had no idea that African cuisine included so many soup recipes, but there they were, night after night, one after the other: peanut soup, lentil soup, cream of mushroom, cream of cauliflower, and curried squash soup. This recipe is my re-creation of the creamy orange liquid that tasted heavenly. The curry powder, I am told, comes from the influence of the many Indians who populate the region, having been brought in by the British during colonial days. Now in their fourth and fifth generations, they are a vital part of the African population.

¼ cup olive oil
1 cup diced shallots
3 whole cloves garlic
¼ cup minced ginger
4 bay leaves
½ teaspoon crushed red pepper
2 ½ pounds butternut squash, peeled and cut
   into chunks
1 ⅓ teaspoons salt
1 teaspoon curry powder
2 cups chicken stock, heated
1-inch chunk palm sugar (available in Asian
   grocery stores)
1 15-ounce can low-fat coconut milk
   freshly chopped chives or fresh curry leaves
   for garnish

**1** In a deep stewpot over medium heat, heat the oil. Add the shallots, stirring for a couple of minutes. Add the garlic cloves and continue to stir as you add the ginger. When the shallots start to soften, about 4 to 5 minutes, add the bay leaves and crushed red pepper, and sauté for an additional minute or 2.

**2** Now add the squash, salt, and curry powder. Stir and cook for 10 minutes or so.

**3** Turn the heat to medium high and add the chicken stock. Put the lid on the pot and bring the soup to a boil. Immediately lower the heat and simmer for an additional 30 minutes, stirring and mashing every 5 minutes. This stirring and mashing will ideally result in reducing the size of the squash chunks. About 15 minutes into the boiling process, add the palm sugar and the coconut milk, and stir.

**4** When the 30 minutes are up, remove all the bay leaves from the soup. With an immersion blender, puree to achieve a creamy texture.

**5** Reheat the soup in its pureed form for 10 to 15 minutes more, adjusting salt to taste, if needed. Garnish with chopped chives or curry leaves just before serving piping hot.
SERVES 6–8

# FISH & SEA-FOOD

## SEA SCALLOPS WITH CRUSHED PEANUTS AND CUCUMBER RELISH

This delicate, elegant dish is also surprisingly easy to make. I stumbled on adding the peanuts because I wanted something crunchy that would offset the soft, voluptuous nature of the sea scallops yet still echo their buttery flavor. This is a dish in which you really have all the basic tastes of salt, sour, hot, and sweet. If you don't have dried mango powder, you can use sumac, or even skip it and just slightly increase the lemon juice in the relish. You can chop up the cucumber and tomato relish beforehand and keep it in the fridge, but don't mix in the peanuts until you are ready to dress the scallops as they will get soggy.

½ cup flour
½ cup finely ground, dry bread crumbs
2 teaspoons dried mango powder
   (amchoor; see page 3)
1 teaspoon cayenne
2 teaspoons fine sea salt
2 pounds fresh sea scallops
2 cups peeled and diced English cucumber
1 cup peeled, seeded, and chopped red and
   yellow heirloom tomatoes
¼ teaspoon brown sugar
½ cup chopped fresh dill
2 to 3 tablespoons fresh-squeezed lime juice
2 to 3 tablespoons olive oil
1 cup dry-roasted peanuts, coarsely crushed
   in a mortar and pestle
   black pepper

**1** In a large glass bowl, mix the flour, bread crumbs, mango powder, cayenne, and ¾ teaspoon of sea salt.

**2** Wash the sea scallops and gently pat them dry with paper towels.

**3** In another big bowl, combine the cucumber, tomatoes, 1¼ teaspoons of sea salt, brown sugar, dill, and lime juice.

**4** Heat the olive oil in a frying pan. While waiting, drop each scallop in the flour mixture, lightly coating all sides.

**5** Sauté the scallops over medium-high heat until they are browned on all their surfaces and cooked through; this should only take about 4 to 5 minutes. If you're using smaller scallops, cook for 3 to 4 minutes. Just before serving, stir the peanuts into the cucumber relish.

**6** Put the scallops on a serving plate and place a generous ladleful of the relish over them. Grind a generous amount of black peppercorns over the top. Serve immediately.
**SERVES 4 AS A MAIN COURSE, 6 AS A STARTER**

## BARBEQUE SHRIMP WITH CHILI HONEY BUTTER

I stopped keeping Chili Honey Butter (page 256) in my fridge because it was just too damn tempting. I'd slather the velvet spread on everything in the pantry. I first spread it on toast, as a way of gussying up breakfast, and then graduated to putting a few pats in the frying pan when making eggs and home fries. Soon I began sautéing beans, fish filets, peas, and whatever other vegetables gave me the excuse to have some of this melted golden bit of heaven in my mouth. Here I give you a simple recipe for barbequed shrimp and grill-charred zucchini ribbons.

2 pounds jumbo shrimp, cleaned, peeled, and
  deveined
¼ cup fresh-squeezed lime juice
⅔ teaspoon salt
2 zucchini (1 pound), blanched for 4 to
  5 minutes, just about halfway cooked, in
  boiling, salted water, and drained on
  paper towels
½ cup Chili Honey Butter (page 256)
4 to 6 wooden skewers, each 1 foot long,
  soaked in cold water for 30 minutes

**1** Marinate the shrimp in the lime juice and salt while readying the grill, approximately 15 to 20 minutes.

**2** Light the grill so that the coals get nice and hot and the flames die down. The coals should be glowing red and white.

**3** While waiting for the grill, use a mandolin or very sharp knife and carefully slice the zucchini vertically into very thin ribbon slices.

**4** Melt the Chili Honey Butter in a small saucepan on very low heat.

**5** To make each skewer, fold a zucchini slice over itself backward and forward to form an accordion shape. Do this by first folding back one end of the zucchini strip (more than an inch) toward the middle of the strip. Now fold it back the other way and then back the other way again. Keep doing this until the strip is completely bunched up, the way one makes a folded paper fan. Pierce the folded zucchini strip and slide it to the end of the skewer.

**6** Now pierce a shrimp through and slide it all the way down the skewer to meet the zucchini. Alternate the shrimps and zucchini on the skewers. You should be able to fit 3 or 4 zucchini slices and 2 or 3 shrimps on a skewer. Don't push the shrimp too tightly up against the zucchini because you want the zucchini to cook through, and if the heat cannot get to it you will have unevenly cooked zucchini (this is also why you first blanch the zucchini).

**7** Now lay the skewers flat and lightly brush both sides with the melted Chili Honey Butter.

**8** Cook the skewers for 2 to 3 minutes on each side. Do not overcook the shrimp or they will become chewy. Two minutes into cooking each side, baste the skewers with the Chili Honey Butter again. Serve warm. SERVES 4

# HOT AND SWEET GRILLED TILAPIA

I love the lip-smacking taste combination of lime, sugar, and salt, pierced with green chili and ginger. These are all the flavors I love in one mouthful. Just whisk these together in a bowl. Once the fish is off the grill, all you have to do is pour on the fresh sauce and serve.

4 6-ounce tilapia fillets
  olive oil
  salt
  freshly ground black pepper
2 tablespoons fresh-squeezed lime juice
2 teaspoons sugar
1 teaspoon minced fresh ginger
1 teaspoon minced fresh green chili (optional)

**1** Take the fillets out of the fridge ½ hour prior to grilling. Brush them on both sides with olive oil, and season with salt and pepper. Brush the grill with olive oil as well, and heat until very hot. The grill should be 2 inches from the heat source.

**2** Combine the lime juice, sugar, ginger, a pinch of salt, and chili (optional) in a bowl.

**3** Place the fish on the grill and cook for 2 to 3 minutes on each side or just until the fish begins to flake. Place the fillets on a plate, and pour the lime and sugar mixture over them. Serve immediately. SERVES 4

# SINGAPORE NOODLES WITH SHRIMP AND SHIITAKE MUSHROOMS

This is my favorite noodle dish. I first tasted a version of it at Mr. Chow's in Los Angeles, and then I had a Filipino version that my housekeeper Ofelia made called pancit. In South India we make a version called semia upma. Chinese and Thai cuisines also have their own noodle dishes, and of course the Japanese have soba and udon. I much prefer rice noodles to other thick noodles because they are more delicate and light on the tongue. The fresh mint and curry powder give off a hot and cool effect in the same bite. When I make these noodles for my cousin Rajni, who is a strict vegetarian (like many in my family), I leave out the shrimp and fish sauce, and it still tastes great.

3 tablespoons sesame oil
1 cup diced onion
1 teaspoon minced garlic
1 tablespoon freshly minced ginger
1 teaspoon minced fresh hot red chili (you can
    also use green serrano chili)
2 tablespoons soy sauce
3 tablespoons Thai or Vietnamese fish sauce
1 pound medium-size shrimp, peeled and
    deveined
1 teaspoon curry powder
2 cups sliced shiitake mushrooms
1 cup shredded carrots
4 ounces cellophane rice noodles (vermicelli
    type), softened per package instructions
1 cup chopped fresh mint

**1** In a large, deep skillet, heat the sesame oil over medium-high heat. When the oil is almost smoking, add the onions, garlic, and ginger. Sauté for 3 to 4 minutes, turn the heat down to medium, and add the fresh chili.

**2** After about 2 minutes, add the mushrooms and carrots, and stir. Then 2 minutes later, add the curry powder and the soy and fish sauces; and 2 minutes later, add the shrimp and stir for 3 to 4 more minutes. Make sure not to overcook the shrimp.

**3** Next, add the rice noodles and toss well to combine all the ingredients.

**4** Now sprinkle the fresh mint over the top. Stir the mint into the noodles just before removing the dish from the heat and serving it at the table. SERVES 6–8

# TAMARIND, GINGER, AND HONEY-GLAZED COD

This is my version of all those miso-glazed cod fillets that are turning up on Japanese menus these days. The tamarind provides a delectable, fruity sour taste. Its gooey consistency makes you want to lick the plate after polishing off the cod. This would also be a lovely glaze for roasting duck or chicken.

1 ounce (golf-ball size) knob of tamarind pulp
  (see page 63)
4 6-ounce cod fillets, skin on
2 tablespoons toasted sesame oil
  freshly ground black pepper
  sea salt
½ cup diced onions
2 tablespoons minced ginger
1 ½ teaspoons honey

**1** Cover the tamarind pulp with 1 ½ cups boiling water, breaking up the mass with a fork or spoon, to make a gravy (see page 63).

**2** Preheat the broiler.

**3** Place the cod fillets, skin sides down, in a broiling pan. Brush the fillets with 1 tablespoon of sesame oil to coat well. Season with crushed black pepper and sea salt to taste and set aside.

**4** In a skillet over medium-high heat, heat the remaining tablespoon of toasted sesame oil. Add the diced onions and sauté for 4 to 5 minutes, and then stir in the ginger. When the onions begin to soften, through a fine-mesh strainer, pour in the tamarind gravy. Reduce the sauce by half to about ¾ cup, and add the honey after 5 minutes. Add salt to taste.

**5** Place the cod in the upper rack to broil for 2 minutes until the fillets just start to color. Remove the cod and turn the oven to 425°F.

**6** Pour the tamarind glaze over the fish fillets, grind some black pepper over them, and return them to the oven, on a high rack. Cook for an additional 5 to 7 minutes, depending on the thickness of the fillets. Serve immediately with noodles, rice, or sautéed vegetables. SERVES 4

# PAN-SEARED FLOUNDER IN CHIPOTLE YOGURT SAUCE

I like flounder for this recipe because it's a mild-tasting fish that soaks up the flavors of the sauce perfectly, but use any white fish you please. The yogurt serves as an excellent sauce base for the fiery chipotle peppers, and the dates give the dish an edge of sweetness that is simply delightful. You can also mix this sauce with some boiled potatoes for a creamy potato salad that is lighter than one made with mayonnaise only. This sauce also works well with pan-seared chicken breasts.

1 ½ cups plain full-fat yogurt (non-fat is fine, too)
⅛ cup light mayonnaise
¼ cup Chipotle and Date Chutney (page 250)
⅛ cup chopped chives
¼ teaspoon salt
3 tablespoons olive oil
¼ cup chopped shallots
1 tablespoon minced fresh ginger
2 ½ pounds flounder fillets

**1** Combine the yogurt, mayonnaise, chutney, chives, and salt.

**2** In a heavy saucepan, heat the oil over medium heat. Add the shallots and ginger. After a few minutes, when the shallots have softened, lay the fish in the pan. Cook each fillet for 2 minutes on each side, taking care when flipping the fish to keep the fillets whole.

**3** Before the fish is done, pour the yogurt sauce into the pan and simmer just until the sauce is heated through. Do not let it boil. Serve straight from pan to plate. SERVES 4–6

# SEAFOOD SPAGHETTINI WITH CHIPOTLE AND GREEN OLIVE PASTE

I find that when I use olive paste and chipotle peppers, this familiar and simple dish takes on an earthy, savory flavor that is more intense than the usual pasta with clam sauce. I was always squeamish about dealing with anchovies, but the paste does all the hard work, and that briny taste is indispensable here. If you don't like clams, you can make the recipe with mussels or smaller cockles, or even leave out the shellfish if you like. It's still amazingly good.

4 cloves garlic, minced
3 medium-size dried chipotle peppers, soaked
 in ½ cup boiling water, drained, minced with
 seeds and skin
2 tablespoons minced capers
1 tablespoon anchovy paste
1 heaping tablespoon green olive paste or tapenade
1 teaspoon dried oregano
1 teaspoon dried thyme
2 large yellow onions, quartered
2 lemons, sliced into rings
7 or 8 bay leaves
1 pound spaghettini
1 tablespoon sea salt
3 tablespoons unsalted butter
½ cup olive oil
2 pounds Manila clams
1 cup chopped fresh flat-leaf parsley

**1** Fill 2 large pots with water and bring them to a boil, one for the pasta and one for the clams.

**2** While the water is coming to a boil, prepare the ingredients for the sauce. In a bowl, combine the garlic, chipotle peppers, capers, anchovy paste, green olive paste, oregano, and thyme.

**3** When the water for the clams boils, add the quartered onions, sliced lemons, and bay leaves. When the water for the pasta boils, add the spaghettini and sea salt, and stir. From here, timing is essential; it is important for the 3 separate processes (clams, spaghettini, sauce) to be ready simultaneously, but whereas the pasta takes 5 to 7 minutes to cook, the clams and sauce need only be heated for 4 minutes.

**4** When approaching serving time, heat the butter and oil in a saucepan over medium-low heat, and sauté the garlic-herb mixture. Now add the clams to the boiling lemon water and stir. Sauté the sauce and cook the clams for 4 minutes—you'll know they're ready when the shells open widely. Do not overcook the clams. Drain the clams in a colander, remove the bay leaves and lemon slices, and add the clams to the sauce, turning off the heat. Stir together to evenly distribute the flavors, and cover.

**5** When the pasta is done just al dente, drain the pasta and mix the sauce, pasta, and parsley together very well. If the pasta seems a bit dry (as it can soak up the moisture of the sauce), you can drizzle a bit of extra virgin olive oil into it while mixing. Serve hot as a main course.

SERVES 4

# RED SNAPPER WITH GREEN APPLE AND MINT CHUTNEY

This crisp, tart chutney is easy to make, as described on page 244. The greatest effort is picking the mint leaves off the stems. The lush, bright green color reminds me of sun-kissed summer meadows. The bite of the chilies is matched perfectly by the sweetness of the apple and the cool, spiky flavor of fresh mint. Red snapper is one of the easiest fish to cook. It has a delicate taste that complements almost anything, and the flaky white texture makes it ideal for sautéing quickly. But any white fish will work amazingly well.

¼ cup fresh-squeezed lime juice
½ teaspoon dried thyme
  salt
4 6-ounce red snapper fillets
1 medium-size onion, sliced in thin crescents
3 tablespoons vegetable oil
2 cups Green Apple and Mint Chutney (page 244)

**1** Combine the lime juice, thyme, and salt (to taste). Marinate the fillets—out of the fridge, for 30 minutes—in this mixture.

**2** Heat a sauté pan over medium-high heat. When the pan is hot enough that you can feel the heat rising from the pan with your palm held 2 or so inches away, add 2 tablespoons of oil.

**3** Pierce each fillet with a fork, letting the fillet hang over the marinade bowl to allow any lime juice to drip off before you put it in the pan—the moisture will splatter, so be careful. Place the fillet in the hot oil, skin side down, and move the pan around so the fillets don't stick. Cook for about 5 minutes, until the skin is crisp. Carefully flip the fillets over and cook for about 2 minutes. Remove them from the pan, and keep them warm in a serving dish.

**4** Add the remaining 1 tablespoon of oil to the pan and toss the onions in it. Sauté for 5 minutes. Add the chutney and cook for 2 to 3 minutes until heated through.

**5** Pour the onion and chutney mixture over the fish. Serve warm. SERVES 4

# FIERY LINGUINE WITH TOMATO AND SHRIMP

When I lived in Milan, we had friends whom we'd visit every weekend from spring to the end of summer in Lerici, a small seaside town near La Spezia in the region of Liguria. I love the food from that part of Italy. It's light and very flavorful. The abundant use of seafood and green herbs (this is where pesto comes from) make it my ideal diet. My friend Michele is a wonderful cook, and always prides himself on using only the freshest fish and seasonal vegetables. He has a garden where he grows everything he needs, from bay leaves to rosemary, oregano, thyme, and lettuces. When we eat this dish, we have no shame. We actually tuck our napkins into our collars and use our fingers as we bite off the shrimp from their tails. We've been known to loudly suck our fingers clean so as not to waste a speck of this glorious spicy tomato sauce.

1 pound large shrimp, peeled and deveined,
   tails on
¼ cup of fresh-squeezed lime juice
2 tablespoons coarse sea salt
2 tablespoons olive oil
4 cloves garlic, crushed
1 orange bell pepper, cut into thin long slivers
3 bay leaves
1 teaspoon dried oregano
¾ teaspoon dried thyme
2 teaspoons crushed red pepper
2 tablespoons drained chopped capers
4 plum tomatoes, cut into 8 pieces each
1 28-ounce can whole peeled tomatoes with juice
2 tablespoons anchovy paste
2 tablespoons butter
1 pound linguine
½ cup chopped flat-leaf parsley

**1** Marinate the shrimp in lime juice and a sprinkle of salt for 15 to 20 minutes.

**2** Fill a large pasta pot with water, and place it over high heat to boil.

**3** Heat the olive oil in a deep skillet over medium heat. Add the garlic and stir-fry for 1 minute. Add the bell pepper, stirring for a couple of minutes, until the pepper slivers soften slightly.

**4** Add the bay leaves, oregano, and thyme. Sauté for 2 more minutes, then add the crushed red pepper and the capers. After 5 more minutes, add the plum tomatoes and sauté for 5 minutes or until the tomatoes begin to lose their shape.

**5** Add the canned tomatoes, stirring and breaking up the tomatoes with a spatula. After 5 to 7 minutes, add the anchovy paste. Simmer and stir for 8 to 10 minutes, adding the butter halfway through.

**6** The pasta water should be at a rolling boil by now. Add salt and the linguine, being careful not to break the pasta. Cook for 8 to 10 minutes, or until done al dente, and drain.

**7** While the pasta cooks, add the shrimp to the tomato sauce. Stir for approximately 3 to 4 minutes, or just until the shrimp is opaque but not overdone; add the parsley.

**8** Drain the pasta from its water and toss with the sauce. Serve hot. Do not add any cheese.

SERVES 4

## SAUTÉED CALAMARI WITH CHECCA

I have a weakness for all things breaded and fried, but it's often a pain to deep fry at home, not to mention hard on the waistline. This recipe is pretty easy to make and doesn't entail the greasy mess of deep frying. I love the salty crunch of sautéed calamari with the tangy juices of tomato and lemon juice. The green touch of parsley gives a bite of freshness that balances the oil and butter, and the jalapeño gives the taste a final zing. Don't bother cleaning and cutting the calamari yourself. It's worth going to a good fishmonger and asking him or her to do all the hard work of dressing the squid into neat rings. Many stores now sell bags of frozen calamari, and these work fine, too. Checca is an Italian word (pronounced kekka) for a chopped tomato and herb salad. Mine is a bit non-traditional because I add jalapeños. But you can leave them out if you like things milder. Serve this dish in cones of brown kitchen or butcher paper, presented on appetizer plates, or, for a rustic touch, on a serving plate lined with newspaper. I sometimes try to find pink Italian sports pages like the Gazzetta Dello Sport or some other foreign-language newspaper, or even those boldly headlined tabloids that talk about alien landings on Earth. It's a fun way to add humor to your table.

1 ½ pounds fresh calamari, cut into rings
1 cup of whole milk
3 tablespoons olive oil
1 tablespoon butter
2 cups dried bread crumbs tossed with
    ½ teaspoon salt
3 cups diced, seeded tomatoes
1 cup chopped flat-leaf parsley or basil
1 or 2 jalapeño peppers, minced
1 teaspoon coarsely ground rock salt
    juice of 1 very ripe lemon

**1** Wash the calamari and dry the rings on paper towels.

**2** Soak the calamari in the milk, mixing with a fork to distribute milk over all of the calamari surfaces.

**3** Melt the olive oil and butter together in a large skillet over medium heat.

**4** Shake the calamari to rid it of excess milk. Toss the calamari in bunches with the seasoned bread crumbs in a brown paper or plastic bag. Shake well to coat all of the calamari.

**5** When the oil and butter are nice and hot, stir-fry the calamari until crispy but not rubbery on the inside, no more than 3 to 4 minutes.

**6** Toss in the tomatoes, parsley, jalapeño, rock salt, and lemon juice. Remove from heat and stir. Serve immediately. SERVES 4–6

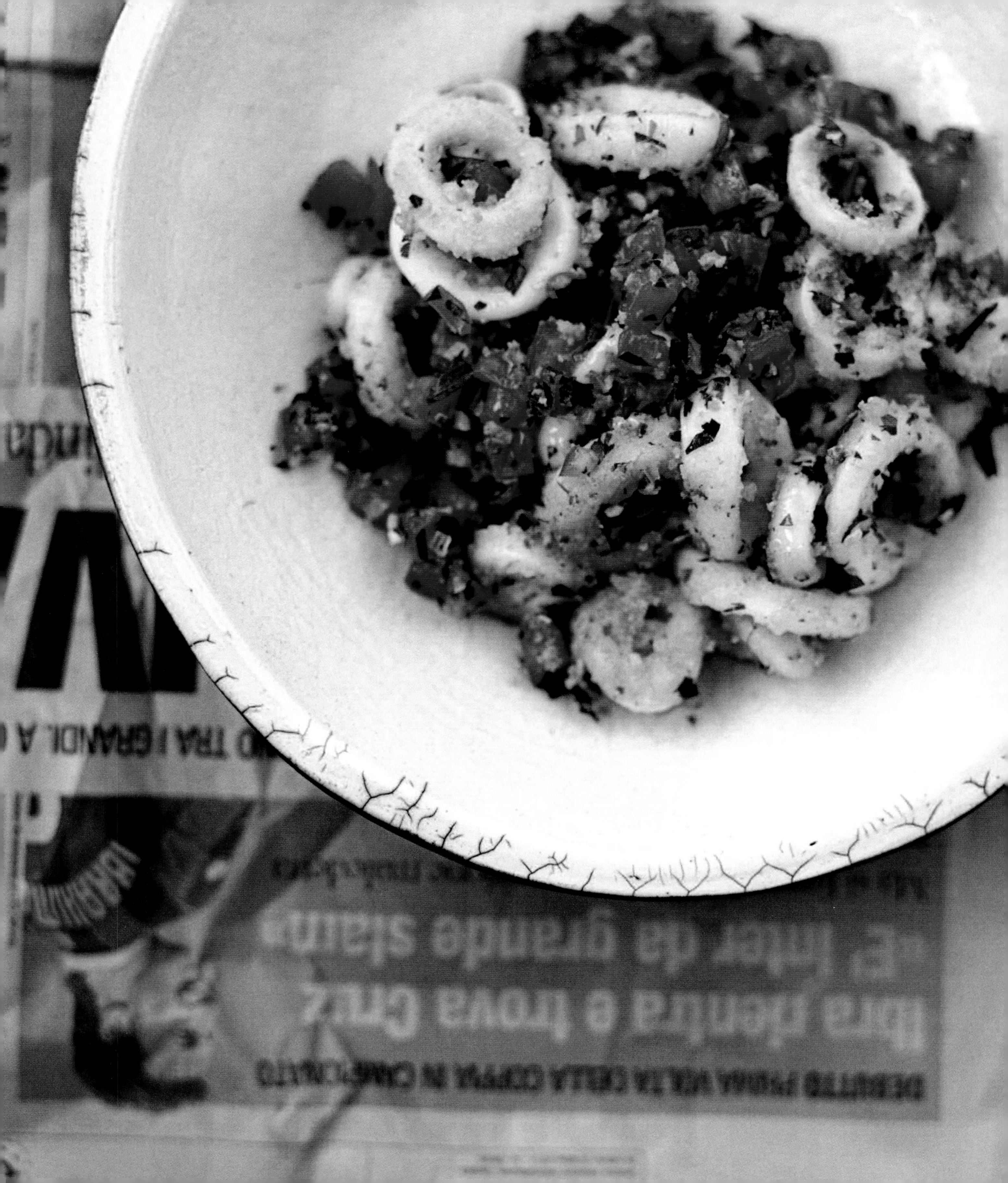

## STEAMED VIETNAMESE MONKFISH, VEGETABLES, AND NOODLES

This is the kind of fish stew I love to eat steaming from a deep bowl balanced on my knees as I sit by the fire on a cold winter's day. You can use any white fish, or even shrimp. My girlfriend Kristin is squeamish about fish, so I often make it for her with chicken, and it is just as divine. Make sure to use chicken stock if you are using poultry instead of fish.

6 tablespoons toasted sesame oil
1 Chinese eggplant (about 8 inches by 2 inches),
    cut into 1-inch slices
4 garlic cloves, peeled
½ cup diced onions
1 ½ tablespoons minced fresh ginger
1 cup diced red bell pepper
1 teaspoon crushed red pepper
1 teaspoon sambar curry powder (or Madras
    curry powder)
6 to 8 fresh kaffir lime leaves
1 13 ½ -ounce can unsweetened coconut
    milk
1/2 pound canned bamboo shoots, drained
    and sliced
2 teaspoons Thai or Vietnamese fish sauce
1 ½ cups fish stock
½ inch square of palm sugar, or ¾ teaspoon
3 ½ ounces vermicelli rice noodles (Lungkow
    is a brand I like)
1 pound monkfish fillets, cut in chunks
½ cup chopped fresh cilantro leaves
2 cups whole baby bok choy

**1** Heat 3 tablespoons of sesame oil over medium heat. Just before the oil begins to smoke, add the eggplant chunks. Sauté over medium-high heat for 7 to10 minutes, or just until the flesh is seared and cooked through. Set aside in a dish.

**2** In a separate, deep skillet, heat the remaining 3 tablespoons of sesame oil. Add the garlic and sauté for 3 minutes. Add the onions, ginger, and bell pepper. Stir for a few minutes, until the bell pepper softens. Add the crushed red pepper, curry powder, kaffir lime leaves, coconut milk, bamboo shoots, fish sauce, and fish stock. Stir.

**3** Add palm sugar and stir. Simmer for a few minutes to let this stew develop into a flavorful broth.

**4** Add the noodles and, after 4 minutes, the fish chunks. Cook just until the fish is done, but not falling apart. Just before removing from the heat, add the sautéed eggplant, and the cilantro and bok choy, and stir for 1 minute before serving. **SERVES 6**

# GREEN DRAGON CURRY WITH SHRIMP

When I'm in London, I often hang out at my friend Alice's place. Her husband, Lars, makes a hodgepodge version of this dish that we call dragon blood curry. I have tried to simplify and defang his fiery version while still bowing to the traditional Thai green curries that are its inspiration. The Vietnamese make a similar curry with noodles called laksa. The blending of fresh herbs gives the dish its fragrance and green color, and the jaggery, or palm sugar, balances the chilies. If you don't have dried mango powder, skip it. I include it in the recipe because the layering of these South Asian ingredients adds to the depth of flavor in the dish.

1 cup roughly chopped shallots
3 garlic cloves, peeled
3 or 4 green serrano chilies
1 tablespoon chopped fresh lemongrass,
   including the bottom portion of the stalk
¼ cup fresh-squeezed lemon juice
1 13 ½ -ounce can unsweetened coconut milk
1 tablespoon minced ginger
1 ¼ cup packed fresh mint leaves
¼ cup fresh basil leaves, ripped apart
1 ¼ cup packed fresh cilantro leaves, stems
   removed
1 tablespoon toasted sesame oil
2 cups Chinese long beans or green beans, cut
   into 1-inch pieces
1 tablespoon fish sauce
5 kaffir lime leaves
1 teaspoon dried mango powder (amchoor; see
   page 3)
1 8-ounce can sliced bamboo shoots, drained
1 ½ cups fish stock
1 inch piece of jaggery (brown cane sugar or
   palm sugar)
1 teaspoon sambar curry powder (or Madras
   curry powder)
¾ teaspoon salt
1 pound medium-size shrimp, cleaned, peeled and deveined

**1** Blend the shallots, garlic, chilies, lemongrass, half the lemon juice, ginger, and half the coconut milk in a food processor. Set this mixture aside in a bowl.

**2** Now puree separately the mint, basil, and cilantro leaves. Add 1 to 2 tablespoons of water, if necessary to help the blending process. Because tender herbs need to be added a bit later so the flavor doesn't cook out in the heat, set this mixture aside.

**3** Heat the sesame oil in a deep skillet over medium-high heat. Add the beans and stir for 5 to 7 minutes. Now add the shallot mixture, the fish sauce, the lime leaves, and the rest of the coconut milk. After 3 minutes, add the mango powder, sprinkling it evenly over the surface of the broth and then stir in well. Turn the heat down to medium and let the sauce simmer for another 5 minutes. Add the bamboo shoots and fish stock. Stir and simmer for another 10 to 12 minutes.

**4** Now add the jaggery, sambar powder, salt, and the mint and cilantro puree, and simmer for another 5 minutes while stirring to melt the jaggery into the broth and marry the flavors together. Now turn the heat to medium-low and add the shrimp. Cook for no more than 4 to 5 minutes, being careful not to overcook the shrimp or they will become chewy. Add in the other half of the lemon juice, taking care not to add any seeds. Stir and serve with plain rice. SERVES 4–6

# WHITE FISH IN COCONUT MILK WITH CURRY LEAVES

This is a quintessential dish of the Malabar Coast in South India. Originally called Meen Moilee, it is said to have been invented for an Englishwoman named Molly who had trouble adjusting to the hot flavors of the subcontinent. Meen is the Tamil and Malayalam word for "fish." If you can't find sambar curry powder, ask for Madras curry powder, but you can also skip it if you'd like the dish to be even more delicate. Molly would have probably preferred it that way, although I love the hint of heat it gives just under the blanket of creamy coconut milk. Serve this dish with simple steamed rice. In India, this dish is made with king fish or other local white fish, so given that the sea bass is under threat, perhaps tilapia and pollack are nice alternatives.

2 pounds wild sea bass or other white fish fillets, washed and dried with paper towels and cut into large chunks
3 tablespoons fresh-squeezed lime juice
2 tablespoons canola or vegetable oil
2 cups thinly sliced shallots
4 garlic cloves, peeled
¼ cup torn fresh curry leaves (about 8 leaves)
3 tablespoons fresh minced ginger
4 fresh serrano or jalapeño chilies, slit or cut in little rings with seeds
1 ½ teaspoons sambar curry powder (or Madras curry powder)
2 cups shredded carrots
1 12-ounce can unsweetened coconut milk
  salt
2 cups roughly chopped fresh cilantro

**1** Marinate the fish in the lime juice for at least 10 minutes and no longer than 30 minutes.

**2** Heat the oil in a large skillet over medium-high heat. Add the shallots, garlic, curry leaves, ginger, and chilies, and sauté until the shallots and curry leaves are wilted. Add the sambar powder and stir. Now add the carrots, and stir for 4 minutes.

**3** Reduce the heat to medium low, and add the coconut milk, stirring vigorously and constantly to prevent the milk from curdling. After 2 minutes, add the salt to taste and 1 cup of water. Stir to mix well; reduce the heat to low. When the oil starts to separate and small pools form on top of the broth, after about 7 to 10 minutes, add the fish with its juices and stir gently so chunks don't break off. Cook for 5 minutes or until the fillets are just cooked and flaky. Turn off the heat, and sprinkle in the cilantro just before serving. SERVES 4–6

# POULTRY

# CHICKEN A LA NUECES DE LA INDIA

I adapted this dish from my friend Carmen. She is a beautiful Cervantes-quoting Mexican writer with big mischievous eyes the color of onyx marbles. The silky texture of ground cashews (called nueces de la India in Spanish) create a sweet buttery molten gold that envelops the chicken and is luscious enough to lick right off the pan.

2 tablespoons olive oil
2 pounds boneless skinless chicken breasts
⅔ cup flour for dusting on a dinner plate
salt and pepper to taste
1 cup roasted unsalted cashews, pureed into powder
3 tablespoons olive oil
3 cloves garlic, minced
1 cup shallots, finely diced
1 teaspoon crushed red pepper
½ teaspoon fresh thyme leaves, chopped
1 ½ cups chicken stock
3 tablespoons honey

**1** Gently pound each breast flat and thin into cutlets, to about 1 inch thickness. Do this by using plastic wrap to cover chicken and pound with a mallet or meat tenderizer, even the back of a heavy metal ladle or large serving spoon will work.

**2** Lightly sprinkle each side of cutlets with salt and pepper.

**3** Heat oil on medium heat in a skillet.

**4** Lightly dredge each side of all chicken pieces in flour to coat with just a light dusting. Shake off any excess.

**5** When oil is hot, sauté chicken single file, don't crowd the pan until lightly browned on both sides, about 2 minutes on each side. When chicken is done, transfer to a large platter, and keep warm and covered.

**FOR THE SAUCE:**

**6** Puree cashews in a blender or processor to form a powder and set aside.

**7** Heat oil on medium heat in another skillet. When oil is hot, sauté garlic and shallots for 2 minutes. Add crushed red pepper and thyme and cook for 1-2 more minutes, just until shallots are glassy.

**8** Pour in the chicken stock. Add honey and stir until this comes to a gentle bubbling boil.

**9** Turn heat to medium low and carefully stir in powdered cashews, stirring vigorously so no clumps are formed. Now turn heat to low, and let the sauce become a gravy-like consistency. Taste and adjust for salt and pepper if needed. Keep the sauce warm on low heat, adding a bit more stock if needed so it doesn't become too thick.

**10** Return chicken to skillet on medium low just until meat is heated through. Now pour sauce over the chicken and serve hot. The chicken can also be plated and the sauce can be poured over that just before serving. **SERVES 6**

# CHICKEN FOR THE BOLD

This recipe is for when you're feeling in need of something lip-smackingly fiery and delicious. It's my ode to all those scrumptious plates of buffalo wings I've consumed over the years. The Chipotle and Date Chutney elevates this traditional dish to death-defying heights of new sophistication. And it's so easy to make that I feel guilty. A word of caution: Serve it only to those who have a high heat threshold. As the name screams, this dish is only for the bold!

½ cup extra virgin olive oil
4 pounds legs and chicken wings
2 cups Chipotle and Date Chutney (page 250)

**1** Preheat the oven to 450°F.

**2** In a large, deep, oven-proof skillet, heat the olive oil and lightly brown the chicken on medium heat.

**3** Add the chutney and cook the chicken for about 10 minutes, turning and basting occasionally. The chicken should be well coated with the chipotle sauce by now.

**4** Once the chicken is cooked through, place it in the oven for 5 to 7 minutes to char the skin a bit and give each piece a baked-on sticky, slightly crispy exterior. Serve hot with lots of napkins! **SERVES 4–6**

# CAST-IRON CHICKEN WITH PRESERVED LEMON

This dish gets most of its zest from preserved lemons. I love the sheen this tangy glaze gives to roasted chicken. It's very easy to preserve your own lemons—really, all you need is salt—but you can buy them at your local Middle Eastern grocery. I use the Moroccan kind for this recipe.

½ cup olive oil
1 whole chicken, approximately 3 to 4 pounds,
   cut into 8 parts
½ cup chopped onion
1 teaspoon minced garlic
½ teaspoon dried thyme
1 teaspoon crushed red pepper
1 whole preserved lemon, diced, with seeds
   removed
2 cups chicken stock
1 cup chopped fresh flat-leaf parsley

**1** Preheat the oven to 450°F.

**2** Heat ¼ cup of the olive oil in a large skillet and brown the chicken, skin side down, on medium-high heat. Don't crowd the pan. When the skin is golden, turn the chicken over to brown the other side. Transfer the skillet to the oven and bake for about 30 minutes, until the chicken is done.

**3** While the chicken is cooking, in a deep skillet heat ¼ cup of olive oil, and brown the onions and garlic. Once the onions have softened, add the thyme, red pepper, and preserved lemon. After 5 minutes, increase the heat and add the chicken stock. Once the stock has come to a boil, reduce the heat and simmer until the chicken is ready to come out of the oven, 25 to 30 minutes. The sauce should by now be very thick and reduced by half. Add the chopped parsley.

**4** Remove the skillet from the oven. Add the sauce and stir to incorporate the pan juices. Serve immediately. SERVES 4

# Careyes, Mexico

I took a trip to Careyes, Mexico, that still haunts me. Careyes is one of the most beautiful spots Mother Nature has ever created, with dramatic, high cliffs overlooking the thundering Pacific Ocean and Eden-like lush landscapes. The terrain produces some of the world's most succulent and tasty fruit. But what I remember most about the trip were the picnics. We packed them on days when we went to untouched white beaches, when we went horseback riding on the most intelligent and pampered of polo ponies, and when we went on endless moonlit adventures.

I say "we," but I mean "he." Every time my companion and I set out for the day's adventures, like Adam and Eve touring the other side of Paradise, our godlike cook, José, would quietly pack a picnic basket and place it gently next to my beach bag. It was the most caring of gestures, and one never asked for. At first it was just tortillas wrapped around leftovers from the prior evening's meal. Then I found sliced fruit and an unusual salad with green chilies and lemon (José had obviously taken note of my extra helpings of salsa at every meal). But soon the meals became more and more elaborate, and included sophisticated desserts and chilled drinks in insulated carafes. The handles of the basket were adorned with flowers and vines picked on the property, and I couldn't help but be wooed by the effort put forth by this macho cook who demonstrated the delicate attention to detail of a young housewife in love.

I befriended José and began to compliment his cooking. I wore down his shyness by asking him pointed questions about his culinary methods or the etymology of the names of certain ingredients. My traveling companion had a low threshold for culinary talk, but I had an endless appetite for it. José seemed not to mind my conversation. At first, it was just to extract the closely guarded recipes that had been in his family for years. Later, it was to tell him that in Indian cooking the same ingredients he used were put to work in other ways. He seemed to take mental note of these ideas and listened intently while chopping the day's vegetables. I found myself enjoying just watching him move about his work as I rattled off recipes of my own. Everything about him made me curious. Like the surrounding jungle, there was a quiet dignity to everything he did. I offered to help him shuck corn, peel onions, make the salad, do anything before each meal that needed doing just to be near him. I was happiest in that kitchen.

He would occasionally get a phone call from a woman, and you could see that it embarrassed him to speak with her in my presence, but my curiosity somehow always overcame my sense of politeness, and I could not bring myself to move out of earshot. His silent, earthy, and hard-working nature was in stark contrast to what I was accustomed to. I would run down the stairs in the mornings, like a child on Christmas, to eagerly see what José had packed for us. I caught him more than once peering at me from behind the kitchen door as I looked into the basket. I began to linger more and more in the kitchen. I watched him butcher things, silently wielding his cleaver high into the air and then bringing it down upon some fish or fowl. One day when he went to the market, I was caught looking for him in the pantry.

As our visit wound down, I found myself saddened that I did not even know José's last name or much about him, so strong was his reserved nature, even in the face of my prying. Most of all, I was saddened by the thought that I would probably never see him again.

On one long, quiet drive, when it was clear to me that my companion and I would be taking no more trips together, he said, "Tell me the truth. You'd rather still be in the kitchen with José, wouldn't you?" "Careyes is such a beautiful place," I said, after a long silence and turned to look out the car window.

# GREEN CHICKEN ENCHILADAS

I love the tart firm flesh of tomatillos, and I am happy to report that they are now widely available. If you cannot find them, try making this recipe with green tomatoes or even firm heirloom tomatoes. Preparing this dish may seem a bit complicated, but all you do is poach the chicken and then use the resulting stock to make a pureed sauce with cooked tomatillos, garlic, and chilies. The chicken enchiladas are baked in a casserole, and the result is well worth the labor. And it's even better when it's reheated the next day with a little extra sauce. I make this dish every May on Cinco de Mayo, and it's always a hit. You can finish preparing these enchiladas hours beforehand, which is just as well because Cinco de Mayo is usually spent having margaritas long before the sun sets, thereby rendering most of us too sloshed and happy to even turn on the oven!

1 pound chicken breasts, skin and bones attached
5 cloves garlic, peeled and left whole
2 bay leaves
1 small Vidalia onion, sliced in half
½ cup chopped fresh flat-leaf parsley
1 tablespoon salt
2 pounds tomatillos, husks removed and quartered
5 to 7 green hot chilies, preferably serrano or jalapeño
2 tablespoons vegetable oil, for frying
5 corn tortillas
4 ounces crumbled queso fresco, queso anejo,
    or crumbled feta cheese
½ cup fresh chopped cilantro, stems removed

**1** Put the chicken breast in a medium-size soup pot and cover it with 8 cups of water. Add 3 cloves of the garlic, the bay leaves, half the onion, all the parsley, and the salt. Cook on medium-low heat for approximately 20 minutes.

**2** While the chicken is cooking, place the 2 remaining garlic cloves, the tomatillos, and the chilies into another pot with enough water to cover the tomatillos. Let this boil for 8 to 10 minutes, until the tomatillos are soft and cooked through.

**3** Dice the remaining onion half.

**4** Drain the boiled tomatillo and garlic mixture in a colander.

**5** Heat 1 tablespoon of oil in a skillet. Add the diced onion and sauté for 2 to 3 minutes, just until the onions become glassy, on medium heat. Add the boiled tomatillos, chili, and garlic, and season with salt. Set aside once the mixture is well mixed and soft, about 5 to 7 minutes.

**6** Remove the chicken from its stock (strain and save the stock!) and shred the chicken when it's cool enough to touch with your hands, discarding the skin and bones.

**7** Put the tomatillo mixture into a blender and blend, adding a bit of the chicken stock, ½ cup at a time, until it resembles a thin gravy or sauce. Transfer the sauce back to a saucepan and simmer for 8 to 10 minutes. Add salt if needed.

**8** Preheat the oven to 375°F.

**9** In a rectangular baking dish, lay each tortilla flat one at a time and fill it with the pulled chicken. Pour about a tablespoon of the tomatillo sauce over the chicken and fold the tortilla closed. Move the first completed enchilada to one side in the dish. Now assemble the next one, and the next one, making sure to distribute the chicken equally among all 5 tortillas. Lay them side by side, so they remain closed.

**10** Pour the tomatillo sauce over the top of the wrapped enchiladas and garnish with cilantro.

**11** Crumble the cheese evenly over the top and cover the dish with aluminum foil. Bake for 10 to 12 minutes, and then broil for 3 to 4 minutes, until the cheese is lightly browned. Serve very warm from the oven. SERVES 4

# TWO HENS LAUGHING

The delicate flavor of Cornish game hens makes this a one-of-a-kind dish that is just right for a special occasion. I used to make it for family gatherings where we would all sit around thinking up names Confucius may have used to describe things. This one stuck.

2 tablespoons canola oil
1 teaspoon black mustard seeds
1 teaspoon fenugreek seeds
1 teaspoon crushed red pepper
½ teaspoon asafetida powder
1 navel orange cut in 8 pieces, peeled and seeded
¼ cup fresh kumquats, halved and seeded
3 cups 1-inch cubes of day-old bread with crusts
¼ cup coarse sea or rock salt
1 tablespoon anar dana (dried pomegranate seeds; optional)
1 tablespoon finely grated orange peel
2 tablespoons honey
2 tablespoons chopped fresh dill
1 tablespoon toasted sesame oil
1 teaspoon cayenne
½ teaspoon sambar curry powder (or Madras curry powder)
2 Cornish game hens, innards removed

**1** Preheat the oven to 350°F.

**2** In a small wok, heat the canola oil over medium-high heat. Add the mustard seeds. When they start to pop and crackle, add the fenugreek seeds, crushed red pepper, and asafetida powder. After 2 to 3 minutes, add orange and kumquat, stir. Cook for 4 to 5 minutes, stirring.

**3** Add cubed bread and just enough salt to taste. Stir-fry the bread and citrus mixture for 4 to 7 more minutes, just until the flavors mix well into a doughy mass. Remove from the heat and stir in the anar dana, if you are using it. Set aside.

**4** Place the orange peel, honey, chopped dill, sesame oil, cayenne, and sambar powder in a bowl; stir together vigorously to form a paste. Set aside.

**5** Wash the hens, and pat them very dry with paper towels.

**6** Rub the skins of the hens very well with sea salt.

**7** Stuff the cavity of the hens with the bread mixture and place them in a baking dish. Cook the hens in the preheated oven. After 7 minutes, turn the pan around for even cooking. After 5 more minutes, remove and glaze hens well with the orange peel paste. Bake for an additional 15–20 minutes, basting often. Uncover for the last 5–7 minutes to roast the skins well.

**8** Scoop out the stuffing; if necessary to cook out any excess moisture, place it in another baking pan and return it to the oven for a few additional minutes. Meanwhile, place the hens facing each other on a large platter, with the legs facing the edge of the platter.

**9** Spoon the stuffing around the birds. Serve hot, and carve tableside. SERVES 4

## SWEET AND SOUR CHICKEN SALAD

I wanted an alternative to the commonly served, mayonnaise-laden chicken salad. This will keep nicely in the fridge, and I dare say is actually better the day after it's made, when it's had time to soak up all the pungent flavors of the chutney and vinegar. Try to find a hot mango chutney (many tend to be too sweet). I like the Sharwood's brand. I add the cayenne to give it an extra peppery push, but you can alter this to suit your taste. You could substitute the Chipotle and Date Chutney (page 250) for the mango chutney, but if you do, reduce the amount by a third and omit the cayenne.

1 pound skinless, boneless chicken breast
2 tablespoons fresh-squeezed lemon juice
   salt
6 strips center-cut bacon
¼ cup mango chutney
⅛ cup olive oil
⅛ cup balsamic vinegar
½ teaspoon cayenne
¼ cup finely diced red onion
1 tablespoon fresh-squeezed lime juice
1 ½ teaspoons chopped capers, rinsed to remove
   excess brine and patted dry with paper towel
4 ounces salad greens, or enough bread
   for 4 sandwiches

**1** Preheat the oven to 400°F.

**2** In a baking dish, drizzle the chicken with the lemon juice, and sprinkle it with a pinch of salt. Cover it, and bake for 30 minutes. Remove it from the oven, and dice the chicken into small chunks.

**3** Cook the bacon strips over medium-low heat until nice and crispy; place them on a paper towel to drain. Slice each piece lengthwise, then chop it into small bits, discarding any fatty pieces.

**4** In a bowl, toss together the chicken, chutney, olive oil, balsamic vinegar, cayenne, onion, lime juice, and capers. Do not add the bacon bits until the dish is ready to serve, as they may become soggy.

**5** Keep the chicken salad in the fridge until ready to serve. Place a scoop of chicken either on top of a mound of greens or on some crusty sourdough or baguette bread. Sprinkle the bacon bits over the chicken and serve. It will keep in the fridge for a couple of days. **SERVES 4**

# CHICKEN KORMA (STEW)

This is another one of those long Indian recipes (this time from the North), and while I like to simplify all things when possible, I am still a stickler for authenticity. Just think of this as a culinary adventure, a trail strewn with beautiful, strange flora, like star anise, green and black cardamom, black peppercorns, and cashews—in short, all things Indian and fragrant.

2 pound boneless, skinless chicken breast, cut into stew chunks
2 tablespoons white wine vinegar
10 green cardamom pods
½ teaspoon black peppercorns
6 cloves
3 whole star anise pods
1-ounce (golf-ball size) knob of tamarind pulp,
    soaked in 1 cup boiling water for 20 minutes
    (see page 66)
4 plum tomatoes, each cut into 8 pieces
2 cups light cream
3 tablespoons sesame oil
3 to 4 dry hot red chilies
1 long cinnamon stick
3 black cardamom pods
1 cup sliced shallots
3 garlic cloves, minced
2 teaspoons minced ginger
½ cup raw cashews, crushed in a mortar and pestle
1 teaspoon garam masala
1 teaspoon salt

**1** Marinate the chicken in the white wine vinegar for ½ hour in the refrigerator.

**2** Remove the seeds from the green cardamom pods and grind these together with the peppercorns, cloves, star anise, and tamarind gravy.

**3** Blend together the tomatoes and cream and set aside.

**4** Heat the oil over medium heat in a deep skillet. Add the red chilies, cinnamon stick, and black cardamom, and stir. After 2 minutes, add the shallots, garlic, ginger, and cashews, and stir for 6 to 8 minutes.

**5** Add the tamarind and ground-spice mixture, and stir for 2 minutes.

**6** Next, add the tomato and cream blend, turning the heat down to medium low. Stir in the garam masala, and cook uncovered for 15 to 20 minutes to cook down the cream and release the flavor of the spices. Season to taste with salt. Toss in the chicken and continue to stir for an additional 7 minutes. Serve on a bed of plain basmati rice. **SERVES 4**

# RED STRIPE CHICKEN

I was once on a photo shoot in Jamaica when the crew and I were invited to have dinner at the house where we had been shooting that day. Our hostess was a retired woman from Washington, D.C., who spent the winter months with her husband playing golf in the Caribbean. The house was set on a hill and had a breathtaking view. The only things that tempted me away from her starlit veranda were the wonderful smells coming from the kitchen. I could not believe that such a sumptuous chicken dish had actually been made with beer—Red Stripe. Her sweet Jamaican cook gave me the recipe in the strongest of singsong accents, and I have tried to reproduce here what I could translate with my ears and decipher with my palate.

2 tablespoons canola oil
2 onions, coarsely chopped
4 whole garlic cloves, peeled
2 green bell peppers, coarsely chopped
3 potatoes, peeled and quartered, about 1 pound
6 carrots, cut coarsely on the diagonal
3 bay leaves
1 tablespoon dried oregano
1 3-pound chicken with a split lemon stuffed
    into its cavity
1 ½ liters Red Stripe or other beer
    salt

**1** In a deep pot, heat the oil. Add the onion, garlic, green peppers, potatoes, carrots, bay leaves, and oregano. Sauté for 5 minutes. Add the entire chicken, turning it to brown on all sides.

**2** Pour the beer into the pot; it should almost cover the chicken. Mix well, and cover the pot. Reduce the heat to medium low.

**3** Intermittently stir and add more beer, if needed to keep the chicken bathed. Add salt and cook until well done, about 45 minutes. Serve in a deep platter surrounded with the vegetables, with the broth poured over the chicken. **SERVES 4–6**

## MOROCCAN BISTEEYA (CURRIED CHICKEN PIE)

Okay, I'll admit that this is probably the most daunting recipe in this book. It all gets easier after you ace this one. I will also say with great conviction that it is the most astoundingly satisfying recipe to execute. I was never so pleased with myself than when I made this pie, and I almost had a tear in my eye when I served it, so beautiful was the result. I have had many bisteeyas in my time, and while the most authentic use ground pigeon, I have saved you from the arduous task of searching for it. Plus you'll find a greater audience for this most grand and deserving of dishes if it's filled with chicken. You could also use ground lamb, and indeed ground turkey, veal, or beef. These flavors are otherworldly and transport one's spirit immediately to the dark and mysterious souks of Marrakech. No matter how complicated this dish appears, it is undeniably worth it.

16 sheets filo dough (17 inches x 12 inches)
3 tablespoons canola oil
1 cup minced shallots
4 cloves garlic, minced
3 tablespoons minced ginger
2 pounds ground chicken
2 tablespoons Worcestershire sauce
2 tablespoons anar dana
(dried pomegranate seeds;
available at Indian grocery stores)
2 cups quartered cherry tomatoes
(retain as much juice and as
many seeds as possible)
2 ½ teaspoons dried mango powder
(amchoor; see page 3)
2 teaspoons curry powder
1 teaspoon salt
4 tablespoons unsalted butter, melted and cooled

GARNISH
2 tablespoons unsalted butter
2 cups slivered almonds
½ teaspoon grated nutmeg
½ teaspoon ground cinnamon
   confectioners' sugar

**1** Remove the filo dough from the fridge and let it sit at room temperature for 30 minutes.

**2** Heat the oil in a large skillet over medium heat. Toss in the shallots, stir for 2 minutes, then add the garlic and ginger. Sauté the ingredients for a few minutes before adding the chicken, breaking it up with the back of a wooden spoon. Add the Worcestershire sauce, stir, and add the pomegranate seeds. Cook, stirring, over medium-high heat for 15 minutes; if the chicken releases a lot of liquid, continue to heat until the juices evaporate. When the meat has browned and just starts to dry out, add the cherry tomatoes, mango powder, curry powder, and salt. Reduce the heat slightly and cook for another 10–15 minutes, stirring vigorously. If the chicken starts to stick to the skillet, add a tablespoon or two of water to help the cooking process. When done, remove from the heat and set aside. Preheat the oven to 425°F.

**3** Prepare the filo dough by laying out a dishcloth on a flat surface large enough to accommodate the flat filo sheets. Lay the filo in a stack on the cloth and cover it with another hand towel. With hot water, dampen and wring out a third hand cloth and lay it flat over the top towel.

**4** Carefully center 1 sheet of the filo over a 12-inch tart pan, allowing the ends to drape over the sides, and push filo gently down into the pan to create a reservoir. Brush it with the melted butter. Do the same for 7 more sheets of filo, for a total of 8, placing each at a 45° angle to the one before it and butter it. The sheets of filo should all have their corners hanging over the edge.

**5** Carefully spoon in the ground chicken filling and fill the pie, smoothing out the filling with the back of the spoon. Center 1 sheet of the filo over the filling, allowing the ends to drape over the sides, and brush it with butter. Do the same with 7 more sheets of the filo, again each layered at about a 45-degree angle to the one below it. Close the pie by carefully folding the draped sheets of filo over the filling. Brush the top with the melted butter.

**6** Bake the pie for 15 minutes. Remove from the oven, and place a flat baking sheet over the pie pan. Carefully flip the pie onto the baking sheet. Brush this side of the pie with butter, and bake for an additional 10–15 minutes, until golden brown.

**7** For the garnish, melt the butter in a skillet over medium heat. Stir in the almonds and cook for 3 minutes. Add the nutmeg and cinnamon, and stir for another 3–4 minutes. Remove the pie from the oven, and pour the almonds over the top of the pie. Sprinkle the confectioners' sugar through a fine sieve (by tapping its sides) over the whole pie. Let the pie cool slightly and settle for about 20 minutes. Serve warm. **SERVES 6**

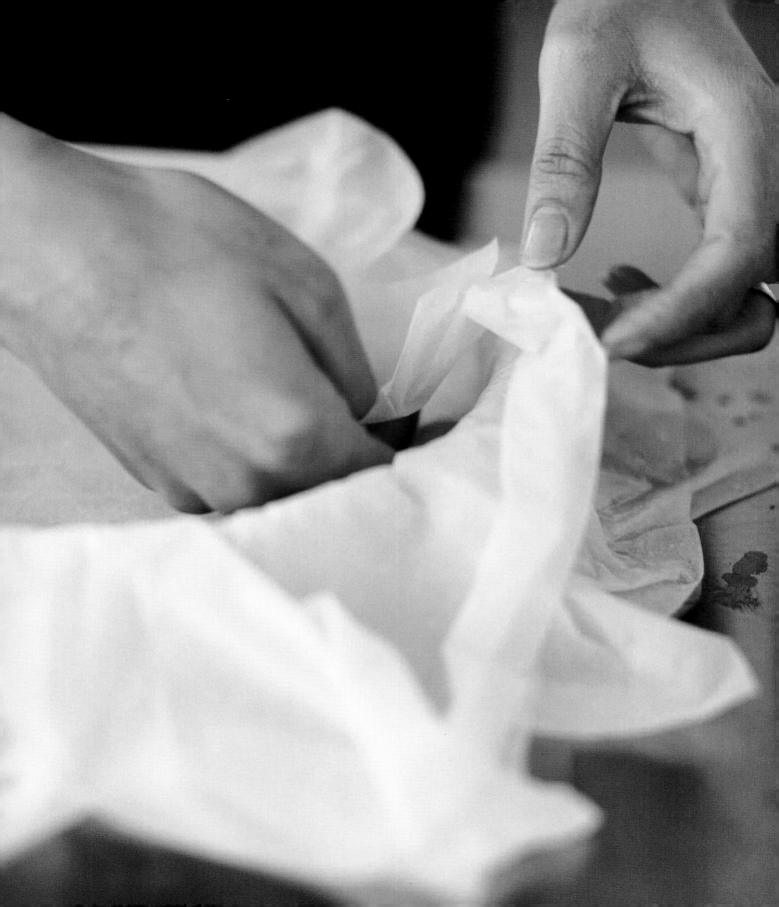

## PIPALI CHICKEN CURRY, MADRAS STYLE

I think I was in Morocco when I first stumbled upon the strange and wonderful
little spice called the pipali pepper. It looks like a tiny, oblong pine cone
and is the color of dry, dark brown bark. Much to my amazement, I learned
that it came from exactly the same part of the world that I do. I asked my
aunts about this strange fruit, and they said it was very commonly used in
regional country cooking decades ago but somehow fell through the cracks
of our family spice basket. The little kernels of prickly heat are so charming
that I suggest you sprinkle a few around roasts and other fall dishes as garnish.
I even use them to decorate my table at Thanksgiving, along with some
cinnamon sticks and star anise. They can be found at all good spice emporiums.
I also use black cardamom, which is twice the size of green cardamom and
has its own special, pungent flavor, with notes of eucalyptus. I apologize in
advance for the long list of ingredients (an unavoidable aspect of some
Indian recipes, I'm afraid), but the end result is well worth it. This dish will
perfume your whole kitchen with the rich, dark aromas of the East. If you
don't have any pipalis around, just use black peppercorns; the women in my
family have been getting away with this substitution for years.

¼ cup sesame oil
5 garlic cloves
2 cups sliced shallots
1 tablespoon pipali peppercorns or
    black peppercorns
3 black cardamom pods
2 ½ tablespoons minced fresh ginger
5 hot, dried red chilis
½ cup shredded unsweetened coconut
1 chicken (3–4 pounds), cut up with giblets
    and skin removed
2 russet potatoes (about 1 ⅓ pounds), peeled
    and cut into 8 pieces each
2 teaspoons curry powder
1 ounce (golf-ball size) knob of tamarind pulp,
    soaked in 1 cup boiling water for 20 minutes
    (see page 63)
10 plum tomatoes, quartered lengthwise
2 teaspoons salt
1 cup chopped cilantro leaves
2 to 3 tablespoons of fresh-squeezed lemon or
    lime juice

**1** Heat the oil on medium heat in a deep stew pot and add the garlic. After 1 minute, add the shallots, and stir well for 3 minutes, until the shallots soften. Now add the pipali peppercorns, cardamom pods, ginger, and dried red chilies. Cook until the onions become wilted and glassy. After approximately 8–10 minutes, add the coconut and stir for 2 more minutes, or until the coconut is toasted.

**2** Add the chicken and stir well to brown all sides. After 3–5 minutes, add the potatoes and curry powder and pour in the tamarind water, straining it through a fine-mesh sieve and pressing the tamarind with the back of a spoon to get out as much of the pulp water as possible. Add 4 cups of warm water through the sieve and stir. Cover and cook for 30 minutes, stirring occasionally.

**3** Turn the heat down to low and add the tomatoes. Continue to stir and cook uncovered for 5 minutes, and then let simmer, covered, for 10–15 minutes. The chicken should be falling off the bone. Adjust salt to taste. Before serving, stir in the cilantro leaves and the lemon juice to awaken the flavors. Serve over plain basmati rice. SERVES 4–6

# KRISPY FRIED CHICKEN

Okay, so what does a girl from South India know about southern fried chicken?
Well, in my defense, for years I've been dutifully following every path
I know to find the best recipe for this beloved favorite dish. Even when I was
a vegetarian, I would break off the coated chicken skin and eat the fatty
bits. The key to moist, plump, juicy fried chicken is the marinating, either in
salted water (brining) or in milk. I've combined the two methods. The
combination of salt and milk results in sheer, succulent pleasure because the
milk makes the meat even sweeter. The second secret is the addition of
Rice Krispies (you can also use corn flakes) and saltines, which creates an
indispensable layered crunch.

2 ½ cups whole milk
5 teaspoons salt
1 4-pound chicken, cut into 8 pieces
1 cup flour
½ cup Rice Krispies, or other puffed
   rice cereal, smashed coarsely
12 saltine crackers, crushed
1 teaspoon dried mango powder
   (amchoor; see page 3) or lemon
   pepper
1 teaspoon cayenne
2 eggs beaten in a shallow bowl
1 ½ cups canola or olive oil
½ pound (2 sticks) butter

**1** Mix the milk and 4 teaspoons of the salt in a large bowl. Add the cut-up chicken and
marinate in the refrigerator for 8 to 10 hours.

**2** Combine the flour, Rice Krispies, saltines, remaining teaspoon of salt, mango powder, and
cayenne. Set aside for dredging the chicken pieces.

**3** In a deep, heavy pan, heat the oil and butter on medium-low heat.

**4** Dredge each chicken piece in the flour mixture and then in the beaten egg. Now dredge
each piece in the flour mixture again, and fry on medium-low heat for 7 to 10 minutes on
each side (7 minutes for wings, 10 minutes for breasts). Do not keep the oil too hot as the
crust will darken and burn before the inside meat is properly cooked. Don't crowd the pan—
cook just enough pieces at a time so that each piece is bathed in oil. Drain on paper towels.
Serve hot with lots of napkins on standby! SERVES 4–6

# MEAT: VEAL PORK BEEF & LAMB

# BBQ KOREAN SHORT RIBS

Is there anything more felicitous than sinking your teeth into a moist beef rib, caramelized to perfection and bursting with smoky, peppery notes? It tingles the tongue in a way that hits all parts of it like an electric current. I love the way the four flavors of sweet, salt, hot, and omami (that's savory to some of us) hit your mouth in one bite. I first stumbled on these luscious, lacquered wands of paradise a few years ago when I went into Koreatown in midtown Manhattan to investigate a bathhouse some of my fashionista friends had discovered. I still go to the bathhouse, and I always revive myself after being pummeled, steamed, oiled, and baked in the sauna for two hours (looking good is exhausting) by sampling one of the many Korean barbeque joints in the neighborhood. My friends roll their eyes, telling me the *point* of going through that kind of medieval torture is to be more svelte, and here I am with a plate of ribs piled high. But I can't resist. My mind never strays from food for long.

2 cups light soy sauce
1 tablespoon toasted sesame oil
1 teaspoon cayenne
2 cloves garlic, minced
½ teaspoon crushed Sichuan pepper (substitute
    plain black peppercorns in a pinch)
1 cup sugar
3 tablespoons canola oil
½ cup chopped fresh chives
½ cup toasted sesame seeds
1 teaspoon dried mango powder (amchoor; see
    page 3)
4 pounds beef short ribs

**1** Mix all ingredients except the ribs in a large bowl. Combine well. Place the ribs in a baking dish and pour the mixture over them. Slather the ribs with your hands to coat them well and evenly with the sauce. Marinate for 2 to 3 hours, covered, at room temperature.

**2** Heat the grill. Place the ribs on the grill rack or barbecue when the coals are glowing red hot and white and the flames have died down, and baste with any leftover sauce. Turn often to cook both sides, until the meat is brown, tender, and caramelized. SERVES 4–6

## ANDOUILLE SAUSAGE WITH BLACK LENTILS AND ARTICHOKES

In the United States, we mostly think of this spicy, smoked pork sausage as part of the Cajun food landscape. It's a major component of gumbo, jambalaya, and other specialties of the bayou. It is so tasty that really all you need to do is pan roast it and wedge it between two pieces of crusty bread. I use it here with lentils and artichokes to infuse a spicy richness that is no less than toothsome.

2 tablespoons olive oil
4 cloves garlic, smashed
1 cup diced cipollini or small yellow onions
10 ounces andouille sausage, sliced diagonally
    into ¼-inch-thick chunks
2 medium-size bay leaves
8 ounces frozen artichoke hearts, quartered
2 tablespoons chopped fresh sage
1 teaspoon dried oregano
½ teaspoon crushed red pepper
4 cups cooked Beluga or other black lentils,
    cooked per package instructions and drained *
2 cups chicken stock
¾ cup buttermilk
1 tablespoon chopped parsley

**1** Heat the oil on medium heat, and when it is hot, but not smoking, add garlic. After 2 minutes add the onions, and after another 2 minutes add the sausage and bay leaves. Cook for an additional 2 minutes (a total of 5 to 7 minutes). Now add the artichokes, sage, oregano, and red pepper, and sauté for 4 to 5 minutes more.

**2** Add the lentils and chicken stock, and cook over medium heat, stirring until the chicken stock reduces almost completely, about 20 minutes.

**3** Reduce the heat to very low, and stir in the buttermilk and parsley. Heat for 2 to 3 minutes until the buttermilk is mixed and heated through. SERVES 4

**NOTE** Beluga lentils are named for their resemblance to the caviar of the same name. You can also use French puy lentils or any other black lentils with great success. Black-eyed peas work, too.

# CARMEN BULLOSA'S SUN-DRIED ANCHO CHILIES STUFFED WITH MEAT AND CAPERS

Ancho chilies are actually dried poblano chilies, just as chipotles are smoked and dried jalapeños. Both start their life very green and turn a deep reddish-brown, or oxblood, color. The flavor of dried anchos can vary quite a bit, so warn your guests. As piquant as they may sometimes be, they still retain a fruity sweetness that is excellent for pairing with meat. This is another dish that I learned from the beautiful and vivacious Carmen B.

6 ancho chilies *
  salt
3 tablespoons olive oil
1 large white onion, chopped
2 garlic cloves, chopped
1 ½ pounds ground beef
½ pound ground pork
½ cup peeled, chopped almonds
20 small capers, drained from brine
5 large green olives, pitted and chopped roughly
1 or 2 healthy pinches cayenne
6 large tomatoes, chopped

**1** Clean the chilies. Slit each one open with a small knife, from top to bottom with one long cut. Be careful not to cut through to the other side of the chili. Make only one opening to form a pocket for the stuffing. Remove the seeds, but keep the stem. Wash each one under water. When they are clean, put them all in cold water with salt for the time it takes the meat to cook.

**2** Heat 2 tablespoons of oil in a deep pot over medium heat. Sauté the onions until they become glassy. Then stir in the garlic, and cook for 1 minute. Stir in the meat and the rest of the ingredients, except the tomatoes. Stir and cook until the meat is completely browned. Let the meat cool.

**3** Take the chilies out of the water and dry them on paper towels.

**4** In a separate pan, heat 1 tablespoon of olive oil and add the tomatoes. Cook until they turn a nice orange color, about 15 minutes; they need to be very well cooked. Add salt to taste.

**5** Preheat the oven to 325°F.

**6** Stuff the chilies, trying to give each one form and body with the meat, and arrange in a baking dish. Pour half of the tomato sauce over them. Be careful not to drown them; it's not soup. Place the dish in the oven for 10–13 minutes. Reheat the remaining tomato sauce, and serve the chilies, with the sauce passed separately. **SERVES 4–6**

**NOTE** Buy the largest, most perfect chilies you can find, with their stems attached. They should measure about 3 to 4 inches.

# LINGUINE WITH WHITE RAGU

I first tasted this creamy white ragu in Venice at Harry's Bar. I try to buy fresh pasta for this dish if I can because this sauce deserves it, but dried pasta also works fine. It's a great way to use veal, too, as it tends to be lighter than beef and more tender. While the sauce is very rich, it still has a delicate flavor that is very refined. This pasta is a meal in itself. If you are against eating veal, turkey or lean beef can be substituted.

2 tablespoons olive oil
1 tablespoon butter
3 medium-size sweet onions, sliced into thin
    crescents*
½ tablespoon dried oregano
2 fresh bay leaves
½ teaspoon crushed red pepper
1 ½ tablespoons balsamic vinegar
1 pound ground veal
1 tablespoon fresh thyme
1 cup heavy cream
3 tablespoons fresh grated pecorino
    cheese
½ cup finely chopped flat-leaf parsley
    salt
1 pound linguine, preferably fresh
1 white truffle, for shaving (optional)

**1** Heat a skillet over medium heat. When it's hot, add the olive oil and butter and, after 2 minutes, the onions, oregano, bay leaves, and red pepper. When the onions begin to wilt, add the vinegar, then the ground veal; stir to separate the veal into tiny bits. Now add the thyme. After the veal is cooked through, about 10 minutes, add the heavy cream and reduce the heat to medium low. Cook this ragu for 20 minutes more and stir occasionally.

**2** Add the cheese and reduce the heat to a low simmer, just enough heat to keep it warm. Stir in the parsley and add salt if needed.

**3** Boil the fresh pasta in salted water for 3 minutes or until just cooked. Drain.

**4** Combine the pasta with the ragu in a large serving dish. Just before serving, shave the white truffle over the pasta, if desired. **SERVES 4**

## NOTE FLAT ONIONS ARE SWEETER

My friend Matt, who comes from a big agricultural family in Modesto, California, gave me this advice about choosing onions: Select the flatter onions, ones that look like they've been pressed down by the hand of Mother Nature, because they're sweeter, and avoid the taller onions that are more oval. Sugar causes the fibers to break down and collapse the onion; therefore, the flatter the onion, the higher its sugar content and the sweeter it will be. Thanks, Matt.

# BRAISED BEEF OR LAMB WITH TOMATO AND CUMIN

As with most stews, the longer you cook this dish, the better it gets. A traditional North Indian recipe—called in Hindi tomater ghost, which literally means "tomatoes and meat"—this dish soothes your shivering and achy body even as you drink in its aroma while it bubbles away on the stove. There are some fiery red chilies in it, but the stew gets its heat from such hallmark Indian spices as cloves, black cardamom, and cumin. If you don't particularly like highly spiced food, you can just cut the chilies a bit, and you'll still find that the aromatic touches of the seeds and pods from the East warm you in the most mellifluous way.

2 tablespoons canola oil
1 teaspoon cumin seeds
2 cups chopped yellow onions
4 large dried whole red chilies
4 cloves garlic, peeled and minced
2 tablespoons minced fresh ginger
3 large bay leaves
2 black cardamom pods
4 cloves
1 ½ pounds beef stew meat or boneless lamb
   shoulder, cut in large chunks
2 ½ pounds plum tomatoes, quartered
1 ½ teaspoons garam masala
   several cups of boiling water
   salt
   sugar (optional)

**1** In a large pot, heat the oil over medium-high heat. Add the cumin seeds, and after 2 minutes, sauté the onions, chilies, garlic, and ginger. Stir-fry for 5 minutes.

**2** Stir in the bay leaves, cardamom, and cloves. Add the beef and stir-fry for 5 more minutes, searing the meat on all sides. Add the tomatoes and the garam masala. Once the tomatoes start to loosen from their skins (about 4 to 5 minutes), turn down the flame, and add enough boiling water to cover the whole mixture. Once it comes to a gentle boil, add a pinch of salt and reduce heat to low. Cover and simmer for 1 ½ hours, stirring every 7 minutes or so, making sure the mixture doesn't stick to the bottom of the pot. You may add additional water, if needed. The end result should be a thick stew gravy and meat so tender it mashes apart with a fork. If the sauce is too sour, add ¼ to ½ teaspoon of sugar to round out the flavor. Mix well. Serve hot over a bed of plain basmati rice, or with oven-toasted flatbread like naan or pita bread. SERVES 4

# PORK WITH CHILE VERDE

This classic Mexican stew uses tomatillos, which are part of the gooseberry family. While you can use green tomatoes in their place (tomatillos must be cooked, whereas green tomatoes need not be), the warm, mellow, flavored sauciness of tomatillos is special and worth experimenting with.

3 tablespoons olive oil
1 ½ pounds pork, cut in large stew chunks
2 medium-size sweet onions, chopped
2 cloves garlic, minced
6 jalapeño chilies, chopped
1 pound fresh tomatillos, quartered
  salt
1 tablespoon dried oregano
1 cup chopped fresh cilantro
juice of 1 ripe lemon (optional)

**1** In a stew pot, heat the oil over medium heat. Add the pork and brown the pieces on all sides. Drain off most of the fat.

**2** Add the onions and sauté until they are glassy, about 4 to 5 minutes. Now add the garlic, chilies, and tomatillos. Stir-fry for 5 minutes.

**3** Add the oregano and stir. Add 2 cups of hot water and bring the mixture to a boil. Reduce the heat to low and simmer covered for about 1 hour. Stir every 15 minutes. Remove from heat and stir in the fresh cilantro. For an extra kick, stir in the lemon juice just before serving.

SERVES 4

# PORK TENDERLOIN WITH DATES AND WATER CHESTNUTS

I frequent an Asian restaurant in London's Notting Hill area called E&O. Correction: I use a restaurant in Notting Hill called E&O as my office. Their gyozas, dumplings with dates and water chestnuts, are the best I've ever tasted. So it is in homage to that lingering taste that I invented this pork tenderloin dish. The sliced tenderloin allows for a shorter cooking time, and for it to be stir-fried on the stove. If you leave the tenderloin whole, bake it covered in the oven instead.

1 ½ pounds pork tenderloin, cut into ½ -inch-thick slices
1 tablespoon ume plum vinegar or rice wine vinegar *
1 to 3 dried chipotle peppers
3 tablespoons sesame oil
1 teaspoon sesame seeds
1 teaspoon cumin seeds
1 cup minced onions
1 tablespoon minced garlic
1 tablespoon minced fresh ginger
1-ounce (golf-ball size) knob of tamarind pulp, soaked in
   1 cup boiling water for 20 minutes (see page 63)
6 dates, pitted and diced
1 cup boiling water
5 ounces canned water chestnuts, drained and sliced
1 teaspoon salt

**1** Place the pork in a bowl, pour in the vinegar, and stir to coat evenly. Set aside.

**2** Soak the chipotle peppers in ½ cup of hot water.

**3** Heat the sesame oil over medium heat in a wok or large frying pan. Throw in the sesame and cumin seeds, and sauté, stirring for 2 minutes. Now add the onions, garlic, and ginger, and stir-fry for 3 to 5 minutes.

**4** Pour in the tamarind water by straining it through a fine-mesh sieve and pressing the tamarind with the back of a spoon to get out as much of the pulp water as possible. Toss in the dates. Heat for an additional 2 minutes.

**5** Drain the chipotle peppers, reserving their soaking water. Chop the peppers.

**6** Add the chipotle water and the cup of boiling water. Stirring often, let this cook down over medium heat to a thick gravy. The sauce will be ready when the oil separates on top to form little pools of oil (about 10 to 15 minutes).

**7** Finally, add the pork, the chipotle peppers, and the water chestnuts; turn the heat up to high. Stir-fry until the meat is nicely glazed (about 5 minutes), adding salt about halfway through. **SERVES 4–6**

**NOTE** Ume plums are Japanese pickled plums that are used to make vinegar and also a syrup that opera singers often drink to coat their throat. Ume plum vinegar is available in gourmet and ethnic markets, but rice or white wine vinegar can be substituted.

## MERGUEZ SAUSAGE WITH FENNEL AND COUSCOUS

This is a meal in itself that doesn't require anything else. I first tasted merguez sausages, which are made with lamb or beef, deep in the souks of Marrakech when I was there years ago for a photo shoot. It's a thin, long sausage that is very spicy and adds incredible flavor to any dish. In 2005, I returned to Morocco to film a remake of *The Ten Commandments*, playing Princess Bithia. The first thing I did was to have a plate of merguez and couscous. Moroccan food is wonderful, with a mix of European, Arab, and African influences. Moroccans use nuts and dried fruits, saffron, preserved lemons, and a number of spices, too. This dish incorporates many of the flavors I love most about this country's cooking. I use harissa, a hot, red chili paste that usually comes in a tube, like toothpaste. It's easy to find in Middle Eastern markets, but you can substitute plain red cayenne for it in a pinch (use the same measurement given below for the harissa.) Merguez is also great to serve when you need a sausage for those who don't eat pork.

1 tablespoon olive oil
1 teaspoon cumin seeds
2 bay leaves
1 cup diced shallots
1 teaspoon dried oregano
8 ½ ounces merguez sausage, cut into 1-inch-
    long pieces
2 cups chopped fresh fennel bulb (discarding
    green stalky tops)
½ teaspoon harissa paste
2 cups chicken stock
⅓ cup dried cranberries
½ cup chopped fresh dill
1 cup couscous
1 teaspoon sumac

**1** Heat the oil over medium heat. Add the cumin seeds and bay leaves; stir, and then add the shallots. Stir-fry for 2 minutes and add the oregano.

**2** Add the sausage and stir-fry for an additional 5 minutes on medium-high heat. Add the fennel and harissa. When grease starts to appear and the meat is dark brown, add the stock. Simmer for 2 minutes.

**3** Add the cranberries and chopped dill. Pour in the couscous, stir well, and turn off the heat. Cover the pot immediately and let the dish steam for 15 to 20 minutes.

**4** If the couscous is not soft and fluffy, sprinkle a couple of teaspoons of boiling stock or water over it, cover, and steam for a few minutes. Be careful not to add too much water. The couscous should not be mushy. Garnish with the sumac. Serve hot or at room temperature. SERVES 4–6

## CASSOULET WITH BEEF

I jokingly call this dish Al Cassoulet (to meld the Arabic and French) because I once had dinner guests who didn't eat pork, not even bacon, or pancetta. They were…a pious lot. I kept prodding my French butcher for a cassoulet recipe that relied only on beef. Of course he treated me like I was crazy, and rattled off an ingredient list that included among other things, a pig's foot. So I put the thought out of my head. But it was late fall and I had a yen to make something nourishing and substantial and I couldn't get over the idea of a big earthenware pot filled with white beans, meat and a thick gravy laden with flavors from the countryside simmering away in my kitchen. As the night of the dinner grew close, I somehow couldn't reconcile my yearning with my butcher's admonishment that, "there was no such thing as a cassoulet without pork." Okay maybe not in France, but here in New York City, where one cannot afford to turn up one's nose at one's various guests' dietary requirements, and cannot bring oneself to turn against some mysterious cooking instinct, improvisation can lead to something that looks and tastes very much like a cassoulet (made without pork). And I wanted to use beef because there is already so much lamb in Middle Eastern cooking. Sorry Maurice. I further have the insolence to add things like omani lemons, and veal stock and dry red chilies. But I assure you that the result is a wonderful cauldron of rich and sumptuous tastes.

1 tablespoon olive oil
4 tablespoons butter
¾ pound veal (rib) chop
2 ½ pounds boneless beef chuck roast, sliced into
   2-inch-thick slices
1 large yellow onion, quartered
1 medium-size red onion, quartered
5 cloves garlic, peeled
5 bay leaves
4 stalks rosemary, each approximately 3 to
   4 inches long, leaves stripped from stems
1 red or yellow bell pepper, coarsely chopped
2 large carrots, cut into 1 ½ -inch pieces
3 whole dry red chilies
1 cup pitted large green olives, preferably Middle
   Eastern ones
7 stalks whole celery, coarsely cut in large chunks,
   including the leaves
1 fennel bulb, quartered
1 ½ tablespoons dried oregano
1 tablespoon marjoram
6 cups veal stock (chicken stock also works)

6 ounces canned tomato paste

2 Omani lemons shattered with a mallet (see page 60)

4 links merguez sausage, about 6 to 8 ounces,
   chopped into bits

2 15-ounce cans white cannelini beans, drained

**1** Heat the olive oil and 2 tablespoons of butter in a skillet over high heat. Sear the veal and the beef for about 1 minute per side. Remove the meat and discard the fat in the pan.

**2** In a large Dutch oven over medium-high heat, melt the remaining 2 tablespoons of butter. Sauté the onions, garlic, bay leaves, and rosemary for 3 to 4 minutes.

**3** Add the bell pepper, carrots, whole dried chilies, olives, celery, and fennel, and stir for an additional 5 minutes.

**4** Add the oregano and the marjoram. After 10 more minutes, add the veal stock with the tomato paste already mixed into it. After 5 minutes, add in the Omani lemons, stirring for a couple of minutes.

**5** Nestle the beef, sausage, and veal in the vegetables, and cover the Dutch oven. Continue to cook over medium to medium-low heat for 2 to 2 ½ hours, until the beef has become tender. Stir every 20 minutes. In the last 15 to 20 minutes, stir in the beans. Serve piping hot.
SERVES 6–8

# VEAL SMOTHERED WITH THYME AND OLIVES

I know we Americans have an aversion to veal because of the much-publicized controversy over farming methods employed by the larger cattle ranches. But now many farms practice a whole new ethos when it comes to raising and feeding veal, and it is possible to eat veal using the same conscience as other meat. This recipe is great with pounded chicken cutlets too.

1 ½ pounds veal scallopini, pounded into 8 flat cutlet pieces
   salt
½ teaspoon freshly ground black pepper
1 cup dry white wine
   olive oil for frying, approximately ½ cup
2 tablespoons butter
3 cloves garlic, cut lengthwise
2 bay leaves
2 ½ cups thinly sliced shallots
¾ teaspoon fresh thyme leaves, stripped from
   their branches
½ teaspoon crushed red pepper
1 cup pitted Spanish green olives
1 cup chicken stock
   flour for dredging, about 2 cups, although
   you may use less

**1** Wash and dry the veal, and sprinkle it evenly with healthy pinches of salt and black pepper. Place the veal in a baking dish, pour the wine over it, and marinate it in the fridge for 3 to 4 hours.

**2** In a deep, wide casserole, heat ¼ cup of oil and the butter on medium heat, and when these are hot and melted together, add the garlic cloves and bay leaves. After 1 minute, add the shallots and thyme, stirring until the shallots are nice and wilted. Add crushed red pepper and salt to taste. Add the olives and the chicken stock. Continue to stir over medium heat, cooking for a total of 5 minutes. Turn the heat down to medium low, and let the mixture simmer and cook down.

**3** Spread the flour evenly on a dinner plate. Carefully remove the veal and pat it dry. Pour the reserved wine marinade into the pot of shallots and olives, and stir; keep heating this pot while browning the veal. Be sure the marinade boils for at least 5 minutes.

**4** Dredge both sides of the veal in the flour.

**5** Heat the oil for frying in a skillet until it is nice and hot. Place the veal in the pan and cook each side for 2 minutes or until lightly browned. Remove the veal from the heat and place it on a serving dish. Depending on the size of your skillet, you may have to do this in batches; don't crowd the pan.

**6** Remove the bay leaves from the shallots and pour the mixture over the veal. Serve immediately. SERVES 4

# In Praise of Bacon

I was a strange child, a vegetarian child, preferring salads to bologna sandwiches, until my mother the Brahmin culinary heretic actually encouraged me to eat meat, much to my disgust at the time.

She was the person who first introduced me to bacon, sometime in the late 70s, initiating a lifetime love affair with crispy American bacon that is only rivaled by my affair with all things fried. (Yes, American bacon. Canadian bacon, is best left, well . . . to the Canadians.)

My mother sprinkled bacon on my salads, on top of eggs and grits and in my grilled cheese sandwiches. I think we may have even dabbled at first with imitation bacon, known in those days as Bacos.

Then, in the late Eighties, my mother recanted, saying I should go back to vegetarianism. Fat chance. By then, I was not only sprinkling bacon on my salads and my grits, I was fanatically ordering club sandwiches in hotels and diners at every stop on our family road trips. I had also started wolfing down bacon Western cheeseburgers after school at Carl Jr.'s. The sublimely pleasurable taste of bacon grease was further enhanced by its mingling with the barbecue sauce, greedily licked off as it dripped down my teenage fingers. I made sure I washed my hands before going home, but like cigarette smoke, my mother could always smell it on me.

In college, the morning after my first keg party, I first made a breakfast of fried eggs and honey mustard glazed bacon on toasted English muffins for the various bodies strewn on the living room floor. Bacon, I can report, is an excellent hangover cure. There's nothing like it to stop the spins. On mornings we were too hungover even to cook, we'd head down to the greasy spoon hangout that I lived atop, Wendy Clark's brunch. So there was always the lingering smell of bacon grease at home, wafting up through the floor-boards and through the pipes.

Ever since those early days I have leapt at any invitation to have bacon. One of my favorite "desert island choices" is surely what I would call an OG (original gansta) of the sandwich world: the BLT. I'm not sure what it is exactly that I love so much. I'm sure the smell of sizzling Hickory smoked pork fat has a lot to do with it. Adding to the appeal is the way the caramelized sugar seeps from the meat, rendering it crunchy and savory, mixing with the sulfates and salt, and mayonnaise. If made with appro-priately crisp, freshly ripped Iceberg lettuce and a thick cut slice of beef-steak tomato still cold from the fridge, it is a delight to be enjoyed with eyes closed.

I cannot muster up the same passion for the thick cut bacon of Europe, although tears of joy do come to my eyes when I think of my first plate of Spaghetti Carbonara. Pancetta only works for me as a substitute for my beloved bacon if it is slowly cooked to miniscule morsels of salty crunchi-ness. I suppose the fact that it is mixed with a quarter pound of pure carbo-hydrates and other deadly fat helps console me from the fact that it is only the distant Mediterranean cousin of my first love: American bacon.

When I lived in Italy, I imagined myself making do like a woman left behind in Sicily, her brave American husband lost at sea, and, after many years, succumbing to the local fare, because, well, we all have needs. In fact I think bacon is the only thing we've got over the Italians.

Recently, in Hawaii while filming the finale of my show, *Top Chef*, our culinary producer Leann Wong decided to show me another use for bacon (as if I needed one?). She baked the most luscious dark, soft velvety chocolate cake laced and studded with bits of . . . you guessed it: bacon. It added a slightly salty undertone with a silken residue of fat not unlike but much more soluble than the traditional lard. Perhaps it just goes down smoother because of the knowledge that it is my one true love. But it also didn't coat your tongue in the way many dishes with lard can. I told her people usually tried to find ways to secretly cut the fat out of chocolate cake, not add fat, much less bacon to it. She fixed me with a death stare as if to say, "I thought you were one of us."

Since doing the show, my eating habits have changed a bit. I eat less and less meat or fatty foods when I'm not filming. But I still make exceptions for bacon. It is still a much-prized secret weapon in my pantry, to use in times of trouble, when I need a little richness and luxury for a particular recipe. In fact, in moments of doubt, my cousin Manu, who has been helping me in the kitchen with these recipes, will often smirk, rub his chin feigning serious thought and say to me, "hmm, why don't you add some bacon? Put some bacon in it, that always works."

All cooks have ingredients they reach for more than they should. Bacon is mine.

# BEEF BRISKET BRAISED IN RED WINE, WRAPPED IN BACON

This is my version of a classic Italian dish called brasato al Barolo made in the Langhe region. This dish is perfect served with some creamy polenta or a serving of mashed potatoes with some of the gravy from the beef drizzled over it. The bacon wrapped around the beef gives it an extra note of silky richness and flavor. I know we're all obsessed with doing things the fastest way possible, but there is merit in slow cooking. This dish is a great example of why.

3 pounds beef brisket
1 750-ml bottle Chianti or Barolo red wine
6 to 8 bay leaves
12 strips center cut bacon
2 teaspoons fresh thyme
4 tablespoons butter
1 red onion, cut into 4–6 wedges
4 carrots, scraped and cut on the diagonal into
   3-inch pieces
2 fennel bulbs, quartered
6 whole celery stalks, cut into 4-inch pieces,
   including all leaves and hearts
8 cloves garlic, peeled

**1** In a bowl, marinate the beef in the wine and bay leaves for 8 to 10 hours in the refrigerator.

**2** In a skillet, cook the bacon over medium heat, being careful not to overcook it—it should not be crispy. Remove the bacon, leaving the fat in the skillet.

**3** Remove the brisket from the wine, saving the marinade. Using the same skillet, turn the heat up to high, and when hot, sear the beef for 1 ½ to 2 minutes on each side, holding the brisket with tongs or a fork to sear all sides.

**4** Place the seared beef in a Dutch oven and let it cool for a couple of minutes. Sprinkle the thyme on both sides of the brisket. Wrap the bacon strips around the brisket, securing them with kitchen string.

**5** Preheat the oven to 300°F.

**6** In the same skillet, melt the butter into the remaining bacon fat, and sauté the onions, carrots, fennel bulbs, celery stalks, and garlic for 4 to 5 minutes to awaken the flavors. Pour the vegetables, the fat in which they're cooked, and the remaining wine marinade over and around the brisket. Cover the Dutch oven and begin the slow cooking process.

**7** Bake the brisket for 3 ½ to 4 hours. Every 30 minutes, remove the brisket and turn it, stirring the vegetables. When done, the brisket should be so tender that you can cut through it with a spoon. Remove the butcher string and bay leaves, spoon the vegetables over the meat and serve. SERVES 4–6

# LAMB MEATBALLS SIMMERED IN CREAMY SPINACH SAUCE

This is a decadent Kashmiri dish, best served in winter to those who like rich Indian curries. Based on a dish called kofta saag curry, it can be made with ground beef, veal, or turkey, as well as lamb. Serve it with steamed basmati rice or an Indian bread, such as naan.

**MEATBALLS**
1 ½ pounds ground lamb
1 egg, beaten
1 teaspoon garam masala
1 tablespoon minced fresh ginger
½ cup minced fresh cilantro
½ to 1 teaspoon cayenne, to taste
1 teaspoon ground coriander seed
1 teaspoon minced garlic
1 cup minced yellow onion
1 teaspoon salt

**SIMMERING SAUCE**
3 tablespoons canola oil, plus extra for greasing
    hands and pan
1 teaspoon cumin seeds
3 whole dried red chilies
3 cloves
4 star anise pods
4 cloves garlic, chopped
1 cup diced yellow onions
1 tablespoon minced fresh ginger
2 cups chopped fresh tomatoes
1 teaspoon sambar curry powder (or Madras
    curry powder)
1 tablespoon tomato paste, dissolved
    in approximately 4 cups boiling water
½ cup beef or chicken stock
1 pound fresh spinach, washed and chopped
    thinly (chiffonade)
1 cup full-fat yogurt
    salt

**1** In a large bowl, combine all the ingredients to make the meatballs, kneading the mixture to a uniform, doughlike consistency.

**2** Rub a few drops of cooking oil into the palms of your hands, so the meat will not stick, and form meatballs about 2 inches in diameter. You will have about 12 to 14 meatballs.

**3** With a bit of oil on a paper towel, rub the inside of a shallow dish to grease it. Place all the meatballs in a single layer, cover them with plastic wrap, and refrigerate them for at least 2 hours.

**4** Remove the meatballs from the fridge and set them on a kitchen counter. To make the sauce, in a large, wide, deep skillet, heat the 3 tablespoons of oil on medium heat. Toss in the cumin, chilies, cloves, and star anise. After 2 minutes, or when the seeds and chilies start to color, add the garlic, onions, and ginger, and stir for 5 to 7 minutes, until the onions become glassy. Then add the fresh tomatoes, and stir until they lose their shape. Add the curry powder and stir to mix evenly.

**5** Add the tomato-paste water and stock, and continue to stir for 3 to 5 more minutes.

**6** With a serving spoon, gently lay all the meatballs into the sauce, pouring a bit of sauce over them to keep them moist. Add enough boiling water to completely bathe the meatballs, if needed. Cover the casserole with its lid, and reduce the heat to medium low. Simmer the meatballs on low heat for 40 minutes, gently stirring often to make sure they remain bathed in sauce and do not stick to the bottom of the pan. Do not break meatballs.

**7** Reduce the heat to low, add the fresh spinach, and cover the pan. Once the spinach has wilted and reduced, about 4 minutes, lift the lid and slowly add the yogurt while carefully stirring. Once all the yogurt has been mixed in, add salt to taste, about ½ teaspoon or so.

**8** Continue to simmer for 10 to 15 minutes more on very low heat until the yogurt starts to separate a bit. Serve hot over plain Basmati rice. SERVES 4–6

# PORK TENDERLOIN WITH ORANGE GLACÉ

I found glistening pieces of orange-peel glacé at Kalustyan's, my local ethnic grocer, and was determined to use them in an innovative way, rather than, as is usually done, in cakes. Fruit glacé is nothing more than candied fruit that hasn't been dried, and thus it retains more of its juicy flavor. Citrus glacé is the type I like best because the acidity balances the sugar required to candy and preserve the fruit. I also use a preserved lemon to balance the sweet glacé, adding a touch of salt and tartness. White wine mellows everything in just the right way.

2 ½ pounds pork tenderloin
1 750-ml bottle Pouilly-Fumé wine
2 tablespoons butter
2 tablespoons olive oil
1 medium-size onion, sliced in crescents
4 cloves garlic, minced
3 carrots, each scraped and chopped into
    4 pieces
1 ½ teaspoons dried oregano
2 cups chopped glacéd orange peel
1 preserved lemon, diced, seeds removed
1 tablespoon fresh marjoram leaves
2 bay leaves
1 teaspoon salt

**1** Marinate the pork in the bottle of Pouilly-Fumé for 1 to 2 hours in the fridge. More time won't hurt.

**2** Preheat the oven to 325°F.

**3** In a skillet over medium heat, melt the butter and oil together.

**4** Remove the pork from the wine marinade and dry it with paper towels. Reserve the marinade. Sear all sides of the pork in the skillet. Place the meat in a Dutch oven.

**5** In the skillet used for searing the pork, sauté the onions, garlic, carrots, and oregano for 3 minutes. Add these vegetables, along with the orange-peel glacé, lemon, marjoram, bay leaves, and salt to the pork in the Dutch oven, and pour in the reserved marinade.

**6** Cover the Dutch oven and place it in the pre-heated oven. Bake for 2 hours, turning the meat and mixing the vegetables every half hour.

**7** Turn off the oven, and let the Dutch oven sit for half an hour while preparing the rest of the meal or eating a first course. Some mashed or roasted potatoes would go nicely alongside this. Place the tenderloin on a platter. Pour what remains in the Dutch oven around the meat and slice the meat tableside. SERVES 4–6

# PAN-ASIAN LETTUCE CUPS WITH CURRIED BEEF

This is a great dish to serve as either a first course or a main course. It's easy to make, and the clean, pure taste of seasoned ground beef with chopped fresh mint and basil is exquisite. In India, we make a similar dish with lamb called keema, which isn't served on lettuce, as is its Thai counterpart. Here I have combined the two cultures' traditional dishes. Of course, you could make this with lamb, turkey, or veal, but I like the flavor of beef best. Letting the flavors of onions, garlic, ginger, and other spices melt into each other on the stove for a longer cooking time is what gives the dish its intense flavor.

2 heads butter lettuce, such as Boston
3 tablespoons canola oil
1 cup diced yellow onions
1 teaspoon minced garlic
1 tablespoon minced ginger
4 green serrano chilies, chopped with seeds
1 ½ pounds ground beef
1 to 2 tablespoons light soy sauce
1 teaspoon curry powder
1 teaspoon dried mango powder (amchoor; see
    page 3)
1 cup roughly chopped fresh mint
1 cup roughly chopped fresh basil
1 ½ tablespoons fresh-squeezed lemon juice
1 tablespoon toasted sesame oil

**1** Carefully separate the leaves of the lettuces to form cups. The firm middle leaves are best; you'll need 6 to 8. Pat dry with paper towels.

**2** In a skillet, heat the canola oil on medium. Sauté the onions, garlic, ginger, and serrano chilies until the onions are glassy, about 5 to 7 minutes.

**3** Add the meat, soy sauce, and curry and mango powders. Cook on medium heat, stirring often to break up the meat into very tiny bits with no lumps. After the spices have been mixed well into the meat, about 5 minutes, turn heat down to medium low and cook for an additional 35 to 40 minutes, until the meat is well cooked and browned. If the meat becomes too dry, a tablespoon or two of water can be stirred into it to keep it moist. Remove from heat.

**4** Stir in the mint, basil, and lemon juice. Spoon the mixture into lettuce cups, and drizzle the toasted sesame oil over the top. Serve warm. SERVES 4–6

# LAMB SHANKS WITH RED WINE AND OLIVES

I usually have to be running a temperature of at least 101°F for my husband to cook anything for me. He did, however, make a mean green tea with honey and hot buttered toast, which he would place at my bedside, while I lay sleeping, when we first moved in together. Now, seven and a half years later, all I can get him to do is microwave some canned soup or leftovers. No matter. He has other very important winning qualities. But suddenly last winter he made a butterflied leg of lamb with red wine. Imagine that.

6 lamb shanks, 3 to 4 pounds total weight
    salt and freshly ground black pepper
2 tablespoons olive oil
1 tablespoon butter
2 cups chopped shallots
4 garlic cloves, peeled
8 medium-size carrots, cut in 1-inch pieces
10 celery stalks, cut in 1-inch pieces
2 or 3 large bay leaves
1 teaspoon dried marjoram
1 teaspoon dried crumbled sage
4 cups frozen artichoke hearts
1 ½ cups pitted large green olives
3 to 4 cups dry red wine, Rioja or Dolcetto

1 Preheat the oven to 300°F.

2 Season the lamb shanks with salt and pepper.

3 In a Dutch oven, melt the olive oil and butter on medium-low heat. Brown the shanks on all sides.

4 Add the shallots, garlic, carrots, and celery. Sauté for 5 minutes. Add the bay leaves, marjoram, and sage. After 2 more minutes, add the artichoke hearts and green olives. Stir well. Finally, pour the red wine over the shanks and stir well. Cover the Dutch oven and transfer it to the preheated over for 1 ¼ to 1 ½ hours, until the meat is tender and falling apart. Serve with buttered rice. SERVES 4

# VEGE-
# TABLES
# & SIDE
# DISHES

## CURRIED CHINESE LONG BEANS WITH BLACK-EYED PEAS

Whenever I first move to a city, I immediately set out to find the nearest Chinatown. There I always find pretty blue and white china bowls, soup spoons and chopsticks, not to mention rice cookers and other gadgets. And I keep going back for the variety of produce, fish—everything, really. These ropey beans are often more than a foot in length, and I sometimes tie them in little knots and then steam and/or sauté them. This recipe works fine with normal string beans, too, but try to find the Chinese kind. I've even seen them at Gelson's supermarkets in California. I've listed the mustard seeds and curry leaves as optional because I don't want you to shy away from this dish if you don't have any around, but they do impart a nice fragrance and flavor, so find them if you can.

2 tablespoons canola oil
1 teaspoon mustard seeds (optional)
2 cups chopped onion
3 cloves garlic, sliced
1 tablespoon minced fresh ginger
12 to 15 fresh curry leaves (optional)
4 plum tomatoes, quartered
1 teaspoon sambar curry powder (or Madras
   curry powder)
1 pound Chinese long beans or green beans, cut
   in 1-inch-long pieces
1 12-ounce can black-eyed peas, drained and
   rinsed
   salt

**1** Heat the oil in a large skillet on medium heat. Add the mustard seeds; when they start to pop and crackle out of the pan, about 3 minutes, add the onion, garlic, ginger, and curry leaves. Cook for 5 minutes, then add the tomatoes, and cook for an additional 5 minutes, for a total of 10 minutes.

**2** Add the long beans. Mix all ingredients well. Add the salt and curry powder. Cook about 20 minutes. Add the black-eyed peas, adjust the salt to taste, and cook for a final 5 minutes or so, just long enough to meld the tastes. Serve hot. SERVES 6

# FIDDLEHEAD FERNS IN GLASSY ONIONS

I first tasted these funny little vegetables in Lancaster, Pennsylvania, in Amish country. Kim, a friend from college, grew up in the rolling hills of this very beautiful part of the country, where fiddleheads grow only in the early spring. They are admittedly more interesting to look at than to taste, but they make such a splash on the plate that I was determined to come up with a recipe for them. They have a similar taste to asparagus but with a bitter edge and are very rich in vitamins. Be careful not to overcook them; they should remain firm to the bite.

2 tablespoons canola oil
½ teaspoon cumin seeds
1 yellow onion, diced
2 cloves garlic, sliced thinly
1 teaspoon crushed dried red pepper
1 pound fresh fiddlehead ferns,
   trimmed and washed
   salt

**1** Heat oil in a skillet on medium heat.

**2** Add the cumin and stir-fry for 2 minutes. Add the onions and stir occasionally until the onions are transparent and glassy, about 5 minutes.

**3** Add the garlic and crushed red pepper; stir well. Finally, add the fiddlehead ferns and sauté for 7 to 10 minutes, until the ferns are cooked but still firm and crisp to the bite. Salt to taste and serve. SERVES 4

# STEFANO'S ROASTED POTATOES

My charming and funny friend Stefano, who moved to America from Italy, has
a weakness for Italian home cooking. Single and hungry, he often shows
up at my home or my friend Franca's, peeking in pots and angling to be fed.
These potatoes are one of his favorite dishes. It's amazing how a few simple
ingredients make the best food possible. This recipe is so easy I wondered
whether even to put it in the book. The balsamic vinegar and pinch of sugar
with sea salt and cayenne give the potatoes a nice, sweet-and-salty edge
that really works. It's still a savory dish, so be careful to just add a pinch of sugar,
no more. It's a trick I use to round out flavors when needed.

1 ½ pounds small new potatoes
3 tablespoons olive oil
1 tablespoon chopped fresh rosemary
⅛ teaspoon sugar (small pinch)
splash balsamic vinegar (about 1 tablespoon)
    pinch cayenne (optional)
½ teaspoon finely ground coarse sea salt

**1** In a deep saucepan, cover the potatoes with cold water, bring to a boil, and simmer for
25 to 30 minutes. Remove the potatoes, and as soon as you can handle them, cut them into
quarters. Lay the potatoes in a single layer in a shallow baking pan.

**2** Preheat the oven to 425°F.

**3** In a bowl, combine and whisk together the oil, rosemary, sugar, balsamic vinegar, and
cayenne.

**4** Drizzle this dressing over the potatoes so they are well covered. You can gently stir the
potatoes a bit to distribute the sauce among the potatoes, but be careful not to break them.
Grind the sea salt over the potatoes.

**5** Place the potatoes in the preheated oven, uncovered. Bake for 20 to 22 minutes, until the
edges are caramelized and a bit crunchy. SERVES 4

# SAUTÉED SWEET POTATO AND LIMA BEANS

I love the taste of smooth, creamy-fleshed sweet potatoes. This eccentric pairing of them with lima beans is a great accompaniment to any meat dish. The recipe is my mother's, and she tells me it's the only way she could get me to eat lima beans when I was a child. If you don't have lima beans on hand, the dish can be made with edamame (soy beans).

1 ½ pounds sweet potatoes
1 pound frozen lima beans
1 ½ teaspoons vegetable oil
1 teaspoon black mustard seeds
1 teaspoon cumin seeds
1 dried whole red chili
1 onion, chopped
2 cloves garlic, sliced
1 tablespoon minced fresh ginger
  salt
2 tablespoons fresh-squeezed lemon or
  lime juice
½ cup fresh chopped cilantro

**1** Boil sweet potatoes, in enough water to just cover them, until tender, about 25 minutes. At the same time, in another saucepan, boil the lima beans in just enough water to cover them, about 15 to 20 minutes. Peel and dice the potatoes once they are cool enough to touch. Drain the lima beans.

**2** In a frying pan, heat the oil over medium heat. Add the mustard seeds; when they pop and start to crackle out of the pan, add the cumin, red chili, onion, garlic, and ginger. Stir well and mix. Let the onion turn golden brown; then add the reserved lima beans and stir. Add the sweet potatoes. Mix all the ingredients well, and sauté for just a few minutes more to mingle tastes evenly. Salt to taste. Add lemon juice and stir. Garnish by sprinkling cilantro over the top. Serve warm. SERVES 6–8

# PUREE OF ROASTED EGGPLANT

I often serve this eggplant as a side dish or as a spread on toasted focaccia bread. It's good, too, alongside barbequed meat. It's a simplified version of an Indian dish called baigan bhartha in Hindi.

olive oil
1 large Italian eggplant, about 1 ½ pounds, halved
    lengthwise
1 red onion, finely diced
3 cloves garlic
2 fresh hot red or green chilies, chopped
½ teaspoon salt
1 cup minced fresh cilantro leaves
2 tablespoons fresh-squeezed lemon juice

**1** Preheat the broiler.

**2** Brush a bit of olive oil on the open cut surfaces of eggplant. Broil the eggplants for 20 minutes, until soft. When they are cool enough to handle, remove the skin and place the pulp in a large bowl.

**3** Mash the pulp; add the onion and stir to combine.

**4** Crush the garlic and red chilies in a mortar with a pestle until a paste is formed.

**5** Add the salt, crushed garlic and chilies, and cilantro (reserving a small amount to garnish the dish) to the eggplant. Blend well.

**6** Squeeze the lemon juice into the mixture, and garnish with the remaining cilantro.
SERVES 4–6. SERVES 8 GENEROUSLY IF USED AS A SPREAD WITH BREAD.

## CAMILLA'S EGGPLANT

Our friend Camie, while very Italian in all her other eating habits, strangely had a prejudice against eggplant. She says she never found it very interesting or tasty. She is obsessed with eating healthily, using only the best organic vegetables and lean meats. A bicycling maniac, she has the best pair of legs I've ever seen—this and a daughter in college. I thought this flavorful dish would be a good accompaniment to her simple grilled fish seasoned with rosemary and lemon. So one golden summer day on Long Island, we made it, tangy with perfectly ripe tomatoes and sun-dried ones. Now my lovely, super-fit friend is a happy convert to this eggplant dish, which is really just a simplified ratatouille.

3 to 4 tablespoons olive oil
4 or 5 large shallots, sliced thinly
½ teaspoon sugar
2 pounds eggplant, cut in large chunks
3 large whole dried red chilies
1 ½ tablespoons fresh thyme leaves
1 teaspoon dried oregano
2 pints grape or cherry tomatoes, halved
½ cup chopped sun-dried tomatoes in oil
2 tablespoons balsamic vinegar
   salt and freshly ground black pepper to taste
½ cup torn fresh basil leaves, stems removed

**1** In a large iron skillet, heat the olive oil on medium heat. Toss in the shallots, and after 2 minutes, sprinkle in the sugar, stirring occasionally. When the shallots are softened and slightly caramelizing at the edges, add the eggplant, dry red chilies, thyme, and oregano.

**2** Cook, stirring, for 15 to 20 minutes.

**3** Add the fresh and dried tomatoes; cook 3 to 5 minutes more.

**4** Add the vinegar, salt, and black pepper to taste. Cook only until the fresh tomato skins are wrinkled, about 5 minutes. Turn off the heat. Stir in the basil, and serve. SERVES 6

# BRAISED SPINACH CATALANA WITH RAISINS AND PINE NUTS

I first had this dish in the center of the old part of Barcelona, while on my honeymoon. I use frozen spinach because it's more convenient; since it cooks down so much it really makes no difference. This is also a great dish to make for unexpected guests—just keep spinach in your freezer.

30 ounces frozen spinach (3 boxes)
2 tablespoons olive oil (maybe a little more)
1 clove garlic, minced
1 medium-size yellow onion, diced
½ teaspoon crushed red pepper
½ cup golden raisins, soaked in 1 cup warm water
    to plump
¼ cup pine nuts
    salt

**1** Defrost the spinach by breaking the frozen bricks into small pieces in a microwaveable dish. Defrost for approximately 9–10 minutes (you can also defrost in a saucepan on the stove, or soak in hot water). Squeeze out the excess water with your hands and set the spinach aside.

**2** Heat the oil in a deep skillet on medium heat. When the oil is hot but not smoking, add the garlic and onion, and stir-fry for 7 to 8 minutes.

**3** Lower the heat to medium-low, add the crushed red pepper, and continue to sauté the mixture for another 5 to 7 minutes, or until the onions are softened and caramelized to a golden brown.

**4** Drain the raisins and add them, along with the pine nuts. Stir-fry for another 5 minutes, until the pine nuts are toasted.

**5** Add the spinach to the skillet and stir to mix well. Add salt to taste and cook, stirring occasionally for 15 to 20 minutes more. You may add additional olive oil if the ingredients stick to the pan. Mash and break up the spinach during this final stage and serve hot.
SERVES 4

## FRESH GREEN BEANS WITH LENTILS AND COCONUT

This classic South Indian vegetable dish is very sophisticated yet quite simple to make. White gram lentils are small, almost the size of a grape seed. When you sauté them in oil, they turn golden brown and crunchy and add an interesting texture to the dish. If you don't have them, you can substitute peanuts or cashew pieces and the dish will be just fine.

2 tablespoons canola oil
1 teaspoon black mustard seeds
2 tablespoons white gram lentils (available in
    Indian markets)
4 whole dried red chilies
1 ½ pounds green beans, cut in 1-inch pieces
½ cup unsweetened shredded coconut
    salt

**1** Heat the oil over medium heat in a large skillet. Add the mustard seeds. When the seeds start to pop and crackle, add the lentils and chilies. Once the lentils are toasted light brown, add the cut beans and stir. Cover and cook for 2 to 3 minutes, stirring occasionally.

**2** Add the coconut and salt to taste. Cook another few minutes while stirring. When the beans are cooked through but still firm and crisp, about 8 to10 minutes, remove from heat. Serve hot. SERVES 4–6

## GREEN MANGO CURRY

This is one of my favorite recipes from childhood. It's a staple at all South Indian weddings, and it was always the dish I looked forward to most at a wedding. It's very easy to make; mostly it's the dicing of the mangoes that takes time. But it is a labor of love worth doing. When I can't find sour mangoes I just look for really firm, hard unripe ones; while their taste is slightly sweeter, they are just as delicious. The curry will keep in the fridge for a few days.

5 large or 8 small green sour mangoes, diced
    super-fine, with skin on but without pit
    salt
1 ½ teaspoons cayenne
2 tablespoons canola oil
½ teaspoon black mustard seeds *
½ teaspoon asafetida powder *
½ tablespoon toasted sesame oil

**1** Place the diced mangoes, salt, and cayenne in a bowl. Set aside.

**2** Heat the canola oil in a large frying pan over medium heat; add the mustard seeds. When they start crackling and popping, add the asafetida powder. Remove from the heat after a minute or two—you don't want the mustard seeds to burn. Pour this sizzling oil mixture on top of the mangoes. Stir to mix the mangoes well with the oil and spices.

**3** Drizzle the toasted sesame oil over the mangoes. The fruit should be crisp and still raw, warmed only slightly by the heat of the oil. Serve at room temperature. SERVES 8

**NOTE** These are found easily at Indian grocery markets.

# GLAZED CARROTS WITH TARRAGON

This dish is a great way to give plain old carrots some pizzazz. The maple syrup brings out the natural sweetness of the carrots, and the tarragon imparts a nice herbal flavor that balances things out. I like to use small, young carrots as they are more tender and flavorful.

2 tablespoons olive oil
1 tablespoon butter
½ cup finely diced onion
1 ½ pounds young carrots, scraped and sliced
  1 inch thick diagonally
⅓ cup loosely packed fresh tarragon
1 ½ teaspoons maple syrup
⅓ teaspoon salt

**1** Heat a deep skillet on medium heat; add the oil and butter. When the butter is melted but not burned, add the onions. Lower the heat if the butter starts to burn, and stir for a couple of minutes.

**2** Add the carrots, and continue to stir for 6 to 7 minutes, depending upon the width of the carrots.

**3** Add the tarragon leaves, ripping them apart as you add them to the skillet. Drizzle the maple syrup into the skillet, add salt to taste, and stir the carrots until they are glazed uniformly, cooking approximately 3 to 4 minutes more. Serve as a side dish. **SERVES 4**

# MEXICAN CORN BREAD WITH JALAPEÑO AND CHORIZO

I love hot corn bread freshly baked out of the oven, with nothing but butter slathered all over it. At some point, I started slicing a piece in half and slipping some prosciutto into it for a mini corn bread sandwich. Then I'd add some cheese and then some hot sauce or jalapeños. Suddenly, I thought, "Wouldn't it be great if all these flavors were baked right in?" The result of that experiment appears below. The sumac is included mainly for color and a bit of tartness, so if you don't have any on hand, don't worry.

1 cup yellow corn meal
1 cup all-purpose flour
½ cup granulated sugar
3 teaspoons baking powder
¼ teaspoon salt
½ teaspoon baking soda
½ teaspoon cayenne
2 large eggs
1 cup whole milk
1 tablespoon olive oil
⅓ cup shredded Monterey jack cheese
½ cup chopped pickled jalapeños
1 15-ounce can whole kernel corn, drained or
   1 pound frozen corn kernels
⅓ cup diced chorizo sausage
2 to 3 tablespoons chopped fresh dill
1 teaspoon sumac (optional)

**1** Preheat the oven to 350°F.

**2** In a large bowl, mix together the corn meal, flour, sugar, baking powder, salt, baking soda, and cayenne.

**3** Separately, in a smaller bowl, thoroughly beat and mix together the eggs, milk, and olive oil. When this mixture is as uniform as possible, add the Monterey Jack cheese, jalapeños and the corn, and mix further.

**4** Add the diced chorizo to the egg and cheese mixture, and mix in. To add this egg mixture to the dry flour mixture, clear the center of the flour bowl to make a well, carefully pour in the egg mixture, and mix together with a fork. You must amalgamate all of the flour, including the powder on the sides of the bowl. Add the dill, and continue to vigorously mix.

**5** Pour this batter into a bundt, round, or square baking pan 8 or 9 inches across, coated with a little olive oil. Bake in the preheated oven for 30 to 35 minutes, or until a toothpick inserted in the center of the bread comes out clean. When done, remove the pan from the oven and allow it to cool for about 20 minutes before carefully flipping the corn bread onto a cake plate.

**6** Just before serving, dust the sumac powder over the top of the bread for some added color and spice. SERVES 8

# SAUTÉED CAULIFLOWER WITH ANISE AND CASHEWS

I love cauliflower, but I usually only have it on a crudités platter or in soup. In North India, in a dish called aloo gobi, it is made with potatoes and cumin. I've replaced the potatoes with cashews and the cumin with anise seeds; it's lighter without the potatoes, and the cashews give it a rich, nutty flavor that pairs well with the anise seeds. The long, dry red chilies give the dish a burst of red color that looks gorgeous on the plate.

2 to 3 tablespoons canola oil
1 teaspoon anise seeds
3 or 4 long dry red chilies
1 cup diced shallots
1 ½ tablespoons minced ginger
2 ¼ pounds cauliflower, broken up into small
  florets
½ teaspoon salt
1 cup cashews

**1** Heat the oil in a skillet over medium-high heat. When it is hot, add the anise seeds and sauté for 2 to 3 minutes.

**2** Roughly break up the chilies, add them to the anise seeds, and stir. After 5 minutes, add the shallots, ginger, and cauliflower. Add ½ cup of water and the salt, and stir. Cook for 10 minutes.

**3** Stir in the cashews, and cook for an additional 10 minutes or so uncovered, until all the moisture is gone, stirring occasionally. The cauliflower will reduce greatly in size, and should have some charred or brown bits at the edges. The cashews should also be toasted brown. Serve hot. SERVES 4–6

## MEXICAN MACARONI AND CHEESE

I adore macaroni and cheese. I could eat a vat of it every day. But, of course, I can't do that, so once in a while, when I really want to treat myself to something rich, creamy, and very comforting, I make macaroni and cheese. It is a very luxurious side dish for any meal, but it's great to make as a casserole when you want to stay in, watch movies all day long, and just lounge around the house. A simple salad is all you need to go with it.

2 tablespoons olive oil
½ cup diced shallots
3 to 4 pickled jalapeños or pickled serrano chilies, minced
½ teaspoon dried Mexican oregano
⅛ to ¼ teaspoon turbinado or raw sugar
8 tablespoons (1 stick) butter
4 cups whole milk
2 cups ditalini or other very small elbow macaroni
1 ⅓ cup grated cheddar cheese
1 cup grated mild jack cheese
3 ounces (approximately ⅓ cup) goat cheese

**1** In a large ovenproof skillet, heat the olive oil over medium heat. Add the shallots and chilies, and stir. After 2 minutes, add the oregano. Lightly sprinkle the raw sugar over the shallots, and stir for 3 minutes. Once the shallots begin to caramelize and lightly brown, turn the heat to low, and add the stick of butter to the pan, chopping it and stirring it in.

**2** After 2 minutes, add the milk and stir. Add the macaroni, and turn the heat back up to medium or medium low, being careful the milk doesn't curdle. After another minute, sprinkle in 1 cup of cheddar cheese and then the mild jack cheese. Stir gently and add the goat cheese, slicing it with your spatula. Continue to stir gently, trying to prevent the cheese from clumping and increasing the heat as you see fit to speed the process. Heat and gently stir for 30 minutes.

**3** Preheat the oven to 350°F.

**4** Remove the skillet from the heat and sprinkle the rest of the cheddar cheese over the top to form a layer. Put the skillet in the oven for 10 minutes, then broil for 3 to 4 minutes, until the cheddar is lightly browned, forming a crust. Serve immediately. SERVES 4–6

## SMASHED POTATO MASALA

This is another old South Indian recipe for a dish called podi mas. My mother always made it when my Uncle Vichu visited us. (I knew who was coming to dinner because of the foods that were prepared.) It's a quick and easy recipe with a taste that's out of this world. The turmeric gives a nice yellow hue to the potatoes, and the white gram lentils give the dish a little crunch, which contrasts nicely with the soft, pillowy texture of the potatoes. If you don't have gram lentils on hand, it's fine to substitute dry-roasted peanuts or raw cashew pieces; even sunflower seeds will work. If you don't want any of these, the dish is still fantastic and is very worth making. Just ask my Uncle Vichu.

1 ½ pounds boiling potatoes
3 tablespoons canola oil
2 ½ tablespoons white gram lentils
1 ½ teaspoons black mustard seeds
2 medium-size onions, diced
3 to 4 fresh serrano or jalapeño peppers, cut in
    rings with seeds
1 tablespoon minced fresh ginger
    salt
1 teaspoon turmeric
1 cup chopped fresh cilantro
2 tablespoons fresh-squeezed lemon juice

**1** Boil the potatoes for about 35 to 40 minutes. Drain them and let them cool. Then peel and quarter them.

**2** In a large pan over medium heat, add the oil and then the gram lentils and mustard seeds. After the seeds start to pop and crackle, add the onions, peppers, and ginger. Stir for 5 minutes. The lentils should be toasted golden brown, and the onions should be glassy. Add potatoes, salt to taste, and turmeric. Smash the potato mixture with a wooden spoon, and mix well so the turmeric gives as even a yellow hue as possible. Remove from heat. Stir in cilantro and lemon juice. Serve hot. SERVES 4

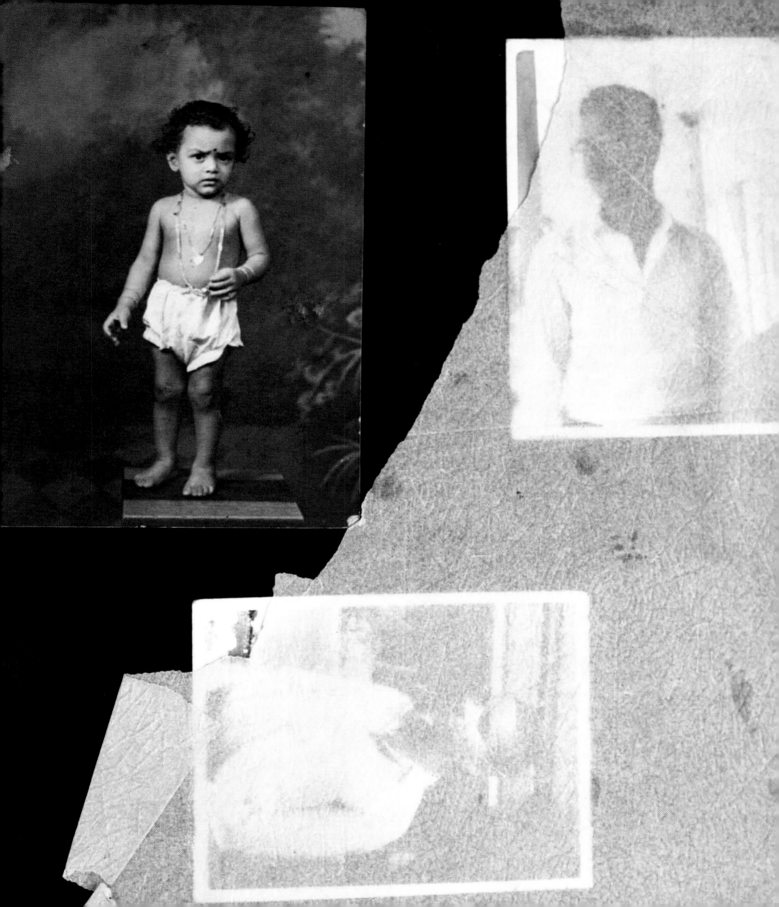

## PAN-CHARRED PEAS

This is one of the first recipes I learned to make, when I was about seven. Much of the flavor in this dish comes from a type of curry powder called garam masala. Most people think curry powder is made up of just one ingredient, or that there's just one type of curry powder made from combining certain spices. The truth is, there are many different types of curry powder, with all kinds of different spices blended together. Most Indian families have their own special recipe or a blend that has been passed down through the generations from cook to cook. Garam masala is the most common spice blend used in North Indian cooking, whereas sambar powder (or Madras curry powder) is used in the South. Curry powders can be made of coriander seed, cinnamon, cloves, cumin, turmeric, black pepper, and many other ingredients all ground up together. Again, the selection and proportions of each ingredient vary from home to home. These peas are a great showcase for the spice blend, and they are very easy to make.

2 tablespoons canola oil
1 ½ pounds frozen small green peas, defrosted
½ teaspoon salt
1 teaspoon garam masala
1 teaspoon anar dana (dried pomegranate seeds; optional)
2 tablespoons fresh-squeezed lemon juice
½ teaspoon chili powder (optional)

**1** Heat the oil in a non-stick skillet over medium-high heat. When the oil is hot, pour in the peas. Cover the skillet for the first 5 to 7 minutes.

**2** Remove the cover, and stir in the salt and garam masala. Sauté for 3 minutes and add the pomegranate seeds, if you are using them. Squeeze in the lemon juice through a sieve. Add the chili powder, and continue to stir until the peas are charred, about 7 to 10 minutes more. Serve hot. **SERVES 4–6**

# ZUCCHINI PUDDING

This Mexican recipe, originally called budin de Calabacita, is adapted from one I learned from my former housekeeper, Lulu. She says this pudding is the only way she can get her daughters to eat any vegetables. The recipe calls for saltines because using them is an easy way of making a crusty topping. Any soda cracker will work fine. This recipe also works well with other squashes and with spinach or boiled cauliflower, though I think zucchini is best.

2 pounds zucchini, chopped
2 fresh bay leaves
8 tablespoons (1 stick) butter, sliced
½ cup snipped fresh dill
1 ½ cups grated mild cheddar cheese
3 ounces soft goat cheese
1 large egg, well beaten
1 cup crushed saltines (about 20 crackers) plus
   10 additional whole crackers
½ cup canned or fresh cooked sweet corn kernels
¼ teaspoon cayenne
   salt and freshly ground black pepper

**1** Boil the zucchini and bay leaves in water for 15 to 20 minutes. Drain and discard the bay leaves.

**2** Preheat the oven to 350°F.

**3** Scatter the butter slices in a 9-inch flat baking or gratin dish.

**4** Add the zucchini to the butter, mashing it in. Stir in the dill.

**5** Add 1 cup of shredded cheddar to the zucchini and continue to stir. Add the goat cheese, beaten egg, crushed saltines (reserving the 10 whole crackers for the top crust), sweet corn, and cayenne.

**6** Crumble the reserved crackers into a bowl and mix with ½ cup of cheddar cheese. Sprinkle this over the top to form a crust. Cover the dish with aluminum foil and bake for 25 minutes, uncovering for the last 5 to 6 minutes so the top browns. The pudding should be bubbling just under the surface. Let it rest in the turned-off oven until ready to serve. Serve hot or warm. SERVES 6–8

# DES-
# SERTS

# BRAISED PLUM GRANITA

There is nothing like biting into the ambrosial flesh of a ripe plum, its juice dripping down one's lips, throat, and hands. It is with the sweet memory of this ecstatic pleasure that I share the following recipe. It's so easy to make that I suggest you buy a bushel of plums at the height of the season, then make a vat of this red-purple liquid to freeze and enjoy all year long. I have written the recipe to accommodate two types of plums, but feel free to use just one or a mix of varieties. In fact, you can even add other stone fruit, like cherries, but the trick is to use fruit that is at the peak of ripeness.

6 succulent plums (3 red/3 black) or wild garden
   plums just about to fall off the tree
1 cup sugar
2 or 3 cloves
1 cup red burgundy wine

**1** Remove the pits, and chop the plums into very small bits, saving as much of the juice as you can. Retain the skin, as it imparts great texture and tartness.

**2** In a deep saucepan, heat the plums, sugar, and cloves over medium heat, turning often to coat the plums well.

**3** After about 5 minutes, slowly add 1 ½ cups water, ¼ cup at a time; reduce the heat to low. Simmer and stir occasionally for 15 minutes.

**4** Add the red wine and simmer for another 20 minutes. If the mixture is too thick, add water, 1 tablespoon at a time.

**5** Pour the mixture into a shallow Pyrex dish. Let it cool. Cover with plastic wrap and freeze for 4 to 6 hours.

**6** Remove the dish from the freezer, and with a long dinner fork, scrape the frozen surface until little pebbles and granules form. Churn the whole mixture quickly so it doesn't melt too much. Then refreeze.

**7** Right before serving, repeat the fork process and spoon the mixture into chilled martini or other cocktail glasses. SERVES 4

# The Universal Joy of Ice Cream

A simple bowl of ice cream inspires a deep, sensual pleasure in just about every-one. What is it about ice cream that brings out the child in us? Is it the rich, creamy, cold velvet that bathes the mouth in a slightly numbing, chilled bliss? Is it the delectable, comforting combination of milk fat, eggs, and sugar, laced with a favorite flavor, that makes us swoon? It is all of that, certainly, but most of all it is because, to truly enjoy ice cream, one must lick it. Whether off a spoon or from atop a graham cracker sugar cone, ice cream begs us to savor and consume it by caressing it with our tongue. It is the most primal method of getting one's most primal need satisfied.

There are no manners for this task; even a child can revel in the act of eating ice cream without fretting about propriety. It makes us, to quote the poem by Anna Swir, "happy as a dog's tail." Even the sternest intellectuals melt when confronted with a bowl of frozen ambrosia. This is how Frederic Prokosch, in his memoir *Voices*, describes one such incident: "That night for dessert we had Singapore Ice Cream, which was studded with ginger and covered with whipped cream. Gertrude Stein looked very voluptuous as she licked her spoon, which she did with half closed eyes, and a slow stately rhythm. Her tongue suggested the bow of an expert fiddler who is playing a languid and delicious adagio."

Ice cream is surprisingly easy to concoct in one's kitchen. Once you have the basic formula, you can add almost anything to it with success. When I bought my first Cuisinart, I began by trying simple concoctions: vanilla, peach, mixed berries, that sort of thing. Then I made chocolate amaretto ice cream, and a lychee and cardamom sorbet that required no eggs or cream at all—just fruit, sugar, water, and a pinch of powdered spice. I even made a rose petal and pistachio ice cream that had not only an unbelievable, layered texture but was so fragrant it reminded me of the rose garlands we used to adorn the goddess Durga's idol in my neighborhood temple in South India.

I found a recipe for red wine ice cream in the paper and tried that, adding raspberries, but was disappointed with the results; the wine curdled the cream somewhat—the result was a ricotta-like mess. To my amazement, however, when I accidentally served it along with my other preparations, an artist friend whose opinion I (usually) respect, loved it. Which goes to show that, as with breading and deep frying, you can puree and freeze just about any sugary thing and people will be happy you have made the effort. And it is very little effort indeed for something that gives as much universal joy as a bowl of ice cream.

# SUGAR AND CINNAMON CHIPS

I once had a friend named Rosario who lived down the street from me. She and I would play until the fireflies came out. We knew it was time to go in when we smelled the humid and salty aroma of her mother frying tortilla chips to accompany her father's evening beer. Rosario's mother would serve his chips plain, along with some serious, chili-infused salsa, and dust ours with sugar and cinnamon. I love these sweet fried snacks because they also remind me of carnival treats we used to eat. They are great crushed over ice cream, or served alongside puddings. Kids love them. And since tortillas last in the fridge for a long time, they are easy to make spontaneously. This method is great if you want plain, homemade tortilla chips, too; just leave out the cinnamon and sugar, and dust with a pinch of salt.

1 teaspoon ground cinnamon
2 teaspoons sugar
8 8-inch flour tortillas
  canola oil for frying

**1** Stir the cinnamon and sugar together thoroughly in a small bowl.

**2** Slice each flour tortilla, as you would a pie, into 6 triangular wedges.

**3** Heat 1 inch of oil in a skillet over medium heat. Line a dinner plate with paper towels.

**4** In the hot oil, fry the tortilla slices, in batches, for about 60 seconds each. Halfway through frying, flip the chips so both sides become golden brown. Using metal tongs or a slotted spatula, remove the chips from the oil and place them on the paper towel to cool and dry for 20 to 30 seconds.

**5** Place the still-warm chips in a brown paper lunch bag, a batch at a time, and add several pinches of the cinnamon and sugar mixture to the bag. Roll the bag closed and shake vigorously to coat each chip with the sweet mixture. Pour the chips onto a serving dish and repeat the entire process. If you prefer, you can sprinkle and toss the chips gently with your hands all at once in a large bowl. Either way, it's important to toss the chips with the sugar and cinnamon while they are still warm, so that they get well coated (which is why I like the brown bag method. Plus it's a nice way to involve kids or anyone else keeping you company in the kitchen). If you're making the salty version, just do the same with salt instead of sugar and cinnamon. SERVES 6–8

# CHOCOLATE AMARETTO ICE CREAM

I am a sucker for a gadget, and while I can go into Chanel and come out empty-handed, I have never been able to get out so easily from a kitchen store. So when I started to write this cookbook, I went out and bought both a deep-fat fryer and an ice cream maker. Then I remembered that while I did have this book to write, I also had photo shoots to do and movies to film, some with very midriff-baring period costumes. So with a heavy heart, not to mention a little of the embarrassment felt by someone who has lived beyond her caloric means, I took the deep-fat fryer back. But I kept the ice cream maker, that little machine that churns out happiness with the tiny vroom, vroom of an engine.

7 ½ ounces bittersweet or semisweet dark chocolate,
   roughly chopped or in chips
2 cups heavy cream
2 cups whole milk
4 large egg yolks
½ cup sugar
1 tablespoon vanilla extract
5 tablespoons Amaretto di Saronno liqueur

**1** Chop 5 ounces of the chocolate in a food processor, taking care not to over-blend as the chocolate will liquefy and stick to the bottom of the processor.

**2** In a medium saucepan, combine the cream, milk, and ground chocolate, and heat for 5 to 8 minutes over medium heat.

**3** In a mixing bowl, combine the egg yolks, sugar, and vanilla extract, and beat until the mixture is smooth and a light yellow color. When the chocolate has melted in the saucepan and the cream sauce is about to boil, reduce the heat to low and stir a few tablespoons of the chocolate mixture into the egg yolk mixture. Gradually add the egg yolk mixture to the cream sauce, stirring continuously so the eggs do not curdle.

**4** After 2 minutes of heating, add the liqueur, and heat and stir for an additional 2 minutes. When the sauce has thickened slightly, cool the mixture completely, either overnight in the refrigerator or in an ice-water bath for 30 minutes.

**5** Stir the cooled cream and pour it into your ice cream maker. Follow the manufacturer's instructions for freezing. When finished, remove the ice cream and place it in the freezer for at least 2 hours to solidify further. About half an hour into this chilling process, remove the ice cream and fold in the remaining 2 ½ ounces of chocolate bits or chips. Place the ice cream back in the freezer, and serve when ready. SERVES 6

## BAKED FIGS WITH MANCHEGO

This turns the simple notion of a cheese and fruit course into something very sophisticated, yet easy to assemble. I love the way the balsamic vinegar caramelizes the fruit, the pepper contrasts with the sweetness of figs, and the savory, melted manchego cheese pulls it all together. I often serve this as a first course, and sometimes I pass it around with drinks, too, and there's a luscious decadence about finishing a meal with something that incorporates all these elements of taste in one glorious bite. If you don't have manchego, substitute any hard, peppery sheep's milk cheese, such as pecorino or caciotta.

12 ripe figs, halved lengthwise
1 to 2 tablespoons balsamic vinegar
1 teaspoon crushed black peppercorns
1 cup grated manchego

**1** Preheat the oven to 350°F.

**2** Lay the fig halves, cut side up, in a baking dish. Brush each lightly with balsamic vinegar, and sprinkle lightly with black pepper and grated cheese.

**3** Bake for 7 to 10 minutes or until just cooked through. The cheese should be lightly toasted on top. Serve immediately. SERVES 8

## PEACHES IN RED WINE

This is a great recipe to whip up on the spur of the moment in summer during peach season. There are many variations of this jewel of a dish, all worth gobbling up. For instance, in the winter, you could use pears and white wine or Moscato dessert wine with cloves. If you have trouble finding the Recioto, which is an Italian dessert wine from Valpolicella, use a dry red wine of your choice and add a sprinkle of sugar, if needed. Port is also an excellent stand-in.

3 cinnamon sticks
5 ripe peaches, peeled, pitted, and quartered
1 ½ cups Recioto red dessert wine or Port

Lay the cinnamon sticks at the bottom of a bowl and place the peaches on top. Pour in the wine, making sure it covers all of the fruit. Marinate in the fridge for at least 2 hours. Serve in small dessert bowls. SERVES 6

# SUGAR AND SPICE COOKIES

These simple cookies are easy to make and fun for kids to decorate. Around my house we always referred to them as tea biscuits, and we dunked them into our strongly brewed and gingery masala chai. They are not as crumbly as shortbread, and are less sweet and a bit harder than most cookies, which is why they're ideal for dunking into tea, coffee, hot chocolate, and warm milk.

2 ¼ cups flour plus extra for dusting the work
  surface
2 teaspoons ground cinnamon
⅔ teaspoon ground cloves
⅛ teaspoon salt
12 tablespoons (1 ½ sticks) unsalted butter
1 ¼ cups sugar
1 large egg
½ teaspoon vanilla extract

**1** Mix the flour, cinnamon, cloves, and salt together.

**2** In a bowl, with a fork or hand-held mixer, combine the butter and sugar, beating until fluffy. Add the egg and vanilla extract.

**3** Add the dry ingredients to the butter mixture, beating until it is well blended into a dough. If the mixture is too dry, add water, ½ teaspoon at a time.

**4** Make 2 flat disks about ½ inch high, and wrap each in plastic. Chill in the fridge, at least 2 hours. Let the disks warm to room temperature for 10 minutes. Further flatten them with a rolling pin to ¼ inch in height, then cut out cookie shapes with cookie cutters or freehand with a knife. If your cookies measure about 2 inches across, you should get about 30 to 35.

**5** Preheat the oven to 325°F. Line 2 baking sheets with parchment paper, or use non-stick cookie sheets.

**6** Arrange the cookies on the baking sheets. Bake for 20–25 minutes, depending on your oven. Turn the baking sheets around once after 10 minutes so the cookies bake evenly. Let them cool. The cookies should be crisp to the bite. They will last up to a week in plastic bags or a cookie jar. MAKES ABOUT 30–35 COOKIES

## CHILLED PAPAYA MOUSSE WITH COINTREAU

This cool, refreshing dessert is easy to make ahead of time and will keep in your fridge for 3 or 4 days. I had only ever had papayas sliced fresh with lemon in the morning or in a blended shake, but I always loved the glowing, pink-orange color of the flesh. Papaya pairs excellently with Cointreau liqueur, and the heavy cream adds to the silky richness of this velvet-smooth dessert. You can serve it in individual martini glasses with a dollop of whipped cream or a few fresh raspberries strewn over the top.

1 large fresh ripe papaya, peeled, seeded, and
  cut into chunks
3 tablespoons plus 1 teaspoon granulated jaggery
  (brown cane sugar or palm sugar)
1 teaspoon vanilla extract
1 ½ cups heavy cream
1 tablespoon Cointreau

**1** In a large saucepan over medium-low heat, combine the papaya, jaggery, and vanilla extract, stirring continuously.

**2** Remove from the heat and, with an immersion blender, puree the mixture to a smooth consistency. Place back on the heat.

**3** Gradually add the heavy cream over 8 minutes, again being sure to continuously stir. Adding the Cointreau after 6 minutes allows it to retain as much of its flavor as possible.

**4** Remove the mixture from the heat and transfer it to a refrigerator-safe container. Cool slightly. Chill the mousse in a fridge overnight so it sets, or until it becomes thick, at least 8 hours. SERVES 6–8

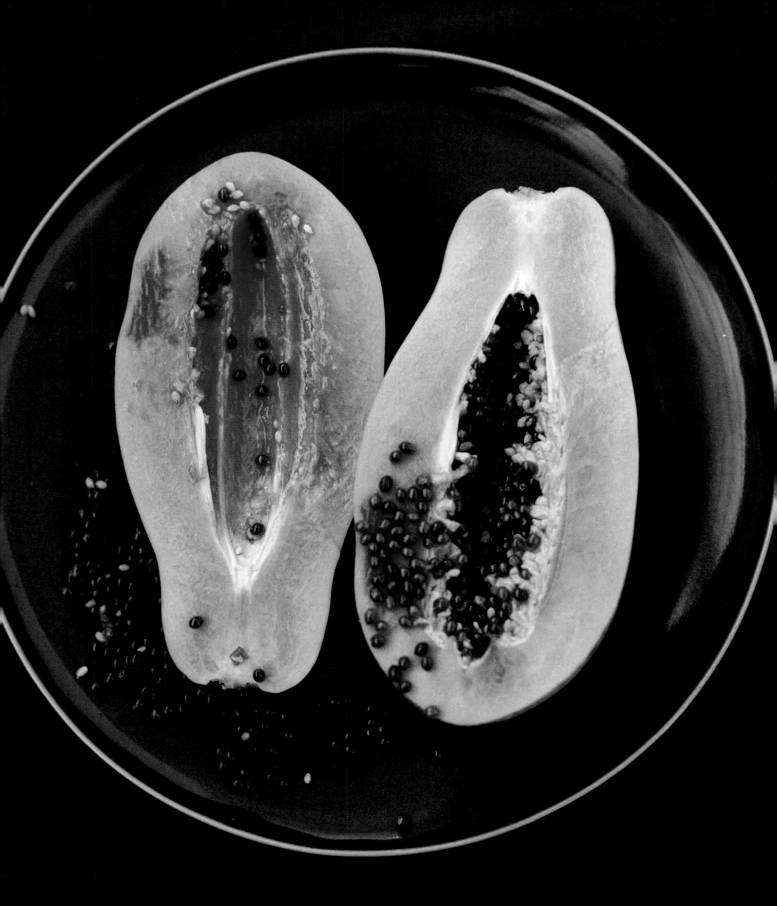

# HONEYCOMB AND FIG ICE CREAM

Honeycomb is available at better food stores and often at farm stands. It is as messy and sticky to handle as one can imagine, but I love using pure honeycomb in a dessert. I first had this ice cream at the Ivy restaurant in London, and I couldn't resist reproducing it in my own kitchen. Make sure you chop the honeycomb into small enough bits and fold them into the cream as it solidifies so that you don't get a big, waxy clump of it in your mouth. Just a tiny bit in each spoonful is enough to give the ice cream a few mysterious, chewy morsels.

2 cups heavy cream
2 cups whole milk
4 large egg yolks
4 teaspoons vanilla extract
½ cup sugar
8 figs or prunes, chopped
6 ounces fresh honeycomb (with honey)

**1** Heat the cream and milk over medium heat for 5 to 8 minutes, until it almost boils.

**2** In a bowl, beat together the egg yolks, vanilla extract, and sugar until the mixture is smooth.

**3** Add 4 tablespoons of the hot cream mixture to the egg yolk mixture, stirring to prevent the eggs from curdling.

**4** Reduce the heat to low, and gradually add the remaining egg yolk mixture to the cream and milk, stirring constantly. Cook for 3 to 5 minutes, until the mixture has thickened slightly. Cool the mixture completely (either overnight in the refrigerator or in an ice-water bath for 30 minutes).

**5** Add the figs or prunes to the chilled ice cream mixture.

**6** Cut the honeycomb into bite-size pieces. Pour the cooled cream into your ice cream maker and follow the manufacturer's instructions. When finished, remove the ice cream and fold in the bits of honeycomb, and stir so all the chunks are evenly distributed. Place it in the freezer for at least 2 hours to solidify further. SERVES 6

# JAMAICAN JOHNNY CAKE

I love the warm, humid smell of fresh bread baking in the oven. Add to that the sweet smell of bananas and molasses with a kiss of vanilla and you have a hoecake that will perfume your home with a luxurious aroma that makes everyone smile. And wait 'til you taste it: sliced still warm from the oven, with just a shake of powdered sugar on top or with vanilla ice cream beside it for dessert; toasted on the griddle and smeared with glistening butter for breakfast the next morning; or even made in muffin pans for easy packing into lunch boxes.

1 cup flour
1 cup fine yellow corn meal
1 teaspoon salt
1 tablespoon baking powder
4 tablespoons unsalted butter, plus extra for
    greasing the pan
½ cup sugar
2 teaspoons vanilla extract
½ cup molasses
2 very ripe bananas, mashed up
1 cup whole milk
2 large eggs, lightly beaten

**1** Preheat oven to 375°F. Place the rack in the middle of the oven. Generously grease a 12-inch by 5-inch loaf pan with a little butter.

**2** In a bowl, mix the flour, corn meal, salt, and baking powder together.

**3** In a separate bowl, blend the butter, sugar, vanilla extract, molasses, and bananas with a hand beater until smooth. Now add the flour mixture and the milk to the sugar mixture. Mix together and then add the eggs, beating until just combined.

**4** Pour the batter into the loaf pan and bake until golden brown—about 40 minutes. Check the cake by inserting a toothpick or fork into the center; if the toothpick comes out clean, the cake is done. Let it cool on a rack. Slice and serve warm. It will keep if wrapped in aluminum foil for a few days. We leave it on the kitchen counter at my house, as putting it in the fridge will dry it out. SERVES 8

# CLOUDS OF CARDAMOM AND CASHEW COOKIES

These wonderful cookies can be made with little effort. The nutty crunch of buttery cashew pieces nestled in the cookies provide a heavenly counterpoint to the fragrant cardamom powder.

½ pound (2 sticks) unsalted butter, chilled and
   cut into 6 pieces
¼ cup confectioners' sugar, plus plenty more for
   dusting
2 cups flour
½ cup raw crushed cashews
2 teaspoons vanilla extract
1 teaspoon cardamom powder
⅛ teaspoon salt

**1** Combine the butter and confectioners' sugar in a bowl to form a stiff mixture. Add the flour, nuts, vanilla, cardamom powder, and salt, and mix well to form a dough. Let stand for 30 minutes, covered, at room temperature.

**2** Preheat the oven to 325°F. Grease a cookie sheet.

**3** Make small balls out of the dough, about 1 inch in diameter, and place them on the cookie sheet. Smash the balls flat with the bottom of a small glass, lightly dipped in flour to prevent sticking, so they resemble irregular clouds. Make sure the cookies don't touch one another.

**4** Bake for approximately 22 to 25 minutes (depending on the oven). Remove from the oven and dust the tops generously with confectioners' sugar. Cool on racks. MAKES ABOUT 25–30 COOKIES, WHICH WILL KEEP FOR A FEW DAYS IN AN AIRTIGHT CONTAINER.

**A SHORT COURSE ON CARDAMOM**

Cardamom comes in two main forms: pale, sage-green pods that contain 8 to 10 tiny, highly perfumed seeds (which are crushed to make the spice powder), and the larger black cardamom that is used to give savory curries and roasts their heat. For baking, make sure you ask for the green kind, as it is significantly more delicate in aroma and taste; the black variety tastes of menthol and eucalyptus. Most supermarkets sell cardamom in its powder form, but it's very easy to make your own freshly ground cardamom powder, for baking and mixing into spiced teas like masala chai. Turkish and Arabic coffee also get their aroma from cardamom; it's a lovely spice to have on hand to dress up many a simple concoction. Just take a dozen or so green cardamom pods (they are only 1/4 inch long) and slowly peel away the pale, dry, green shell of each to reveal the tiny, black, pellet seeds inside. One side of the pod will be more pointed; with your thumb and index finger, peel back a side by breaking the little pointed nub. You can even smash or crush a few at a time with the back of a large metal spoon or ladle. Make sure you have a small mortar and pestle on hand; peel the pods directly over the mortar's basin so as to catch all the seeds. Once you've collected enough seeds, discard the green outer shells, and pound the seeds into a fine powder with the pestle. Save in a small glass jar in your pantry; the powder will keep its fragrance for months if you seal it well.

# GREEN APPLE AND PLUM CRUMBLE

There are three different types of sugar in this recipe, not to mention the sugar that coats the Frosted Flakes cereal (known to my English stepson as Frosties). It's the layers of different types of sugar that complement the tart and tangy acidity of the Granny Smith apples and the plums. If you don't have all these different types of sugar, don't fret; the crumble will still come out well. I just like layering them, and let's face it, when was the last time you got to use all these pantry ingredients in one pan? If you don't have Frosted Flakes (which probably means you don't have children), you can use regular corn flakes and just sprinkle on an additional ¼ teaspoon of sugar. I love using the cereal as it adds to the crunch of the crust. Plus I get a tiny shiver of satisfaction when I use things I have around the kitchen in unorthodox ways. It makes me feel a little like MacGyver, the guy on that old TV show who could make bombs out of rubber bands and wine corks.

2 Granny Smith apples, peeled, cored and diced
1 cup pitted, diced fresh plums
1 tablespoon orange juice
2 tablespoons granulated sugar
1 tablespoon turbinado or raw sugar
1 tablespoon dark brown sugar
½ tablespoon ground cinnamon
2 pinches clove powder
2 ½ tablespoons flour
1 tablespoon butter, chilled and cut into pieces
¼ cup crushed Frosted Flakes
   vanilla ice cream to serve on the side

**1** Preheat the oven to 375°F.

**2** In a medium bowl, mix the apples, plums, orange juice, ½ tablespoon of dark brown sugar, 1 tablespoon of granulated sugar, and all the turbinado or raw sugar, the cinnamon, and the clove powder.

**3** In a separate medium-size bowl, mix the flour, the rest of the sugars, and the butter. Cut it all up with two knives until it forms a crumbly mixture. Then add the Frosted Flakes and mix well.

**4** In a shallow, 8-inch, ovenproof baking dish, spread the apple mixture evenly. Then distribute the flour mixture over the top to form a crust that entirely covers the fruit.

**5** Bake uncovered for 40 minutes. If the dish is not golden brown and bubbly at the end of this time, increase the oven temperature to 400°F for an additional 5 minutes. Serve it piping hot with a side of vanilla ice cream. SERVES 4

# TUSCAN LEMON PUDDING

This is one of the first recipes I learned to make when I lived in Italy. It's a simple, creamy pudding that is ladled from a large bowl into little cups and eaten unadorned with a spoon, at room temperature or cold. There is a tiny restaurant in my old neighborhood in Brera, Milan, called Latteria San Marco, where there are only six tables and they take no reservations. Maria, who runs the front of the restaurant, gave me this recipe more than a decade ago, and it is still a crowd pleaser. It can also be used to fill cannolis, and in Naples and other parts of southern Italy, you will find it in those pastries. But there is nothing more comforting than a good bowl of old-fashioned pudding.

5 large eggs
1 quart whole milk
6 tablespoons sugar
  grated zest of 1 lemon
  cookies or wafers for dipping (optional)

**1** Prepare a bagna Maria, or cold-water bath, by filling a stoppered sink with ice-cold water. I usually add a bowl of ice cubes to keep it really cold.

**2** In a bowl, beat the eggs with a hand-held beater until they are well combined and frothy.

**3** In a large saucepan, heat the milk, sugar, and lemon zest over medium to medium-low heat, stirring constantly with a wooden spoon. When the sugar is dissolved, slowly add the eggs, being sure to stir constantly to keep the texture smooth and even. Raise the heat a tiny bit to speed the process, if necessary, but never stop stirring, as the eggs may scramble; having the heat too high will also cause the eggs to scramble, so be careful. You will know the pudding is done when the spoon is coated; about 20 minutes of constant, patient, gentle stirring will do the trick. Remove the pan from the heat, and move it straight to the cold-water bath, placing the saucepan in the sink, being careful not to immerse the pan so deeply that water from the bath gets into it. Stir until the mixture is cooled and thickens even more.

**4** Transfer the pudding to a serving bowl and refrigerate for 4 to 6 hours, covered with plastic wrap. Serve with cookies or wafers for dipping. SERVES 8

# PINEAPPLE AND POMEGRANATE CRUMBLE

I love the tie-dyed effect of the ruby-colored pomegranate juices leaking all over the sunshine-yellow flesh of pineapple in this very old-fashioned dessert. You can use almost any fruit to make a crumble, so if you're out of pomegranates or just don't feel like taking the time to peel them, use dried cranberries, or fresh cherries, or raspberries. You can even add a few frozen blueberries to contribute to the color and flavor of this dessert. It's fun to have a crumble-making session for kids on the dining room table with all kinds of fruit. Remember to lay down newspaper first and place all the ingredients in bowls. Each child can make individual-size crumbles in small, oven-safe dishes or ramekins. Another great way to make individual crumbles is to use a muffin tin. Again, don't worry if you haven't got all the types of sugars; it'll still be fun, and delicious to boot.

16 ounces canned or fresh pineapple chunks, reserving the juice
1 cup fresh pomegranate seeds, free of white pith
    (see page 8)
⅛ teaspoon ground cinnamon
    a healthy pinch of ground cloves
2 tablespoons granulated sugar
2 tablespoons dark brown sugar
2 tablespoons turbinado or raw sugar
3 tablespoons flour
2 tablespoons unsalted butter, plus extra to coat
    pan
2 tablespoons Frosted Flakes, or corn flakes with
    ¼ teaspoon sugar added
    vanilla ice cream for serving on the side

**1** Preheat the oven to 375°F.

**2** In a bowl, mix together the drained pineapple, pomegranate seeds, cinnamon, cloves, and 1 tablespoon each of the granulated sugar, the dark brown sugar, and the raw sugar. Add 1 tablespoon of the reserved pineapple juice and set this mixture aside.

**3** In another bowl, cream the flour and butter with 1 tablespoon each of the 3 sugars; this can be done with 2 sharp knives. Further mash the mixture into a coarse meal with a fork. Now add the Frosted Flakes and mash together.

**4** Butter a shallow, 6-inch baking dish. Spoon in the fruit mixture and press down with the back of a tablespoon to distribute it evenly. Top with the flour and Frosted Flakes mixture. Cover with foil and bake for 45 minutes, removing the foil in the last 5 to 10 minutes to brown the crust. If not golden brown and bubbly by the end of the cooking time, turn the heat up to 400° F for an extra 5 minutes. Allow to cool and set for several minutes, but serve warm with cold vanilla ice cream. SERVES 4

# LYCHEE GRANITA

If I had to pick only one dessert I would be allowed to eat for the rest of my life it would be this frozen amber nectar. Let me save you from totally unnecessary labor. I have tried this recipe with fresh lychees, traveling on the subway to Chinatown, procuring them after much indecipherable bilingual chatter, and painstakingly peeling their pine cone shells away, pitting them, and taking great care not to lose a drop of their juice. And I have made it with a can of lychees I got from the Korean deli on the corner. Dear reader, the result is the same. This recipe is so easy that even a seven-year-old child could make it, and what's great is that it will keep in your fridge for weeks. Just rake the surface to shave off enough to fill a small bowl. It's an exotic twist on those shaved-ice snow cones of childhood. If you don't have turbinado or raw sugar, just use plain sugar. Don't give yourself any reason not to make this scrumptious dessert.

¼ cup turbinado or raw sugar
30 ounces canned lychees in heavy syrup
⅛ cup dark brown sugar
1 ½ teaspoons cardamom powder

**1** In a deep pot, boil 2 cups of water with raw sugar, stirring until the sugar is dissolved. Add the lychees with their syrup, the dark brown sugar, and the cardamom powder. Reduce the heat to low, and simmer for 12 minutes.

**2** Pulse-blend the ingredients with an immersion hand blender for 5 seconds at a time to blend the lychees into a coarse pulp; be careful not to blend the ingredients too smooth or evenly, as there should be chunks left in the sorbet.

**3** Pour the mixture into a freezer-safe shallow pan, let it cool slightly, cover it with plastic wrap, and freeze it for at least 12 hours. During the freezing process, mix up the granita by raking the surface with a fork after 4 hours to keep the solid bits suspended.

**4** To serve, remove the pan from the freezer and, using a sturdy dinner fork, rake the frozen veneer of the mixture to break up the ice into pebbles and grains. Serve immediately in chilled cups. The granita should keep for 3 to 4 weeks if stored, covered, in a freezer.
SERVES 6–8.*

**NOTE** The granita tends to melt very quickly, so if I'm serving a large group, I nestle each serving cup in a larger bowl with crushed ice in it. This keeps the granita chilled a bit longer at the table. If you have an ice cream maker, you can pour the chillled mixture into it for a smooth sorbet.

# POCHETTES OF CARDAMOM CRÈME ANGLAISE

I can't hide the fact that this pastry is a bit laborious, but it is also a spectacular feat of kitchen artistry. It is so impressive on the plate that people won't believe you made this at home. You can make the crème anglais ahead of time, even the day before, and later just assemble the pochettes in the muffin pan and bake. Before you remove them from the pan let them set a bit and cool so they will keep their shape. I like to use non-stick muffin pans, but if you'd rather not, then make sure to butter the pan generously. You can also do a variation of these pastries by making one large round pastry, as in the bisteeya recipe on page 126, using a round tart or pie pan. Once again, let it cool and settle so that it takes form before cutting into it. If you are daunted by the pastry part, just make the crème anglais, which is wonderfully sinful on its own or for dipping cookies into, and great alongside the Jamaican Johnny Cake (page 213). The recipe for the crème anglais below will serve 4 to 6 people on its own. You'll need only a cup and a half for the pochettes, so you'll have enough for a second dessert for 4 people for the next meal. I stumbled into making these pochettes when I had filo pastry left over from the bisteeya recipe.

CRÈME ANGLAISE
2 cups light cream
2 cups heavy cream
1 ½ cups sugar
⅔ teaspoon cardamom powder
½ teaspoon vanilla extract
8 large eggs

POCHETTES
1 package filo dough (about 30 sheets, 17 inches
   by 12 inches)
8 tablespoons (1 stick) butter, clarified
3 tablespoons confectioners' sugar

FOR CRÈME ANGLAISE

**1** Heat the light and heavy cream in a heavy-bottomed saucepan over low heat and mix in the sugar. Stir gently to help dissolve the sugar, and add the cardamom powder and vanilla extract. Simmer gently for 20 minutes.

**2** Beat the eggs and gradually add to the cream mixture, stirring constantly for about 10 minutes so the eggs don't scramble.

**3** In a stoppered sink, prepare a bagna Maria, or ice-water bath, deep enough to surround the saucepan, but shallow enough that the saucepan can rest on the sink bottom. When the cream mixture has thickened into a rich sauce, remove the pan from the heat and immediately place it in the ice-water bath to shock the cream and thicken it further. Gently stir for some time until the mixture thickens slightly. Serve warm or at room temperature, or refrigerate and serve cold.

FOR POCHETTES

**1** Remove the filo dough from the refrigerator 30 minutes before using.

**2** Lay out a dishcloth on a flat surface large enough to accommodate the filo sheets. Lay 20 to 22 sheets of filo in a stack on the cloth (18 are needed, but it's good to have a few extra ready for mishaps). Quickly cut the filo sheets into 6-inch squares; it's easiest to do this with kitchen shears. Immediately cover the squares with another hand towel. With hot water, dampen and wring out a third dishcloth and lay it flat over the second one. This is to keep the filo from drying out.

**3** Preheat the oven to 375°F.

**4** Remove 3 squares of the filo at a time, leaving the rest under the hand towels. Take 1 square and brush it with the clarified butter. Place a second square of the filo at a 45-degree angle over the first, and brush it with butter. Place the third sheet at a 45-degree angle over the second and brush it with butter.

**5** Place each filo stack into a muffin-tin cup and gently press down on the center to form a bowl, being careful not to tear the fragile dough.

**6** Spoon 2–3 tablespoons of the cooled crème anglaise into each muffin cup (for a total of 1 1/4 cups). Gather together the corners of the filo and close the pochette, twisting it gently into a rose floret. Peel down the petals to fan out a nice crown. Brush the top of the pochette with the clarified butter. Repeat this until you have 6 pochettes, and bake them for 15 to 20 minutes. Remove when the tops are browned nicely. Let the pochettes cool and sprinkle the confectioners' sugar over the tops. Serve warm or at room temperature. **SERVES 6**

**NOTE** THE CRÈME ANGLAISE WILL SERVE 4–6 IF SERVED ON ITS OWN, AND STILL SERVE 3 OR 4 AFTER REMOVING THE 1¼ CUPS FOR THE POCHETTES .

# The Rose Witch

When I was growing up, before my mother had the nice garden she has now, we lived in a two-bedroom apartment like college roommates. She had just moved us from New York to California, something I vehemently held against her for years. Fresh from her second divorce, my mother sought a better life for us out West, where the rents were undeniably lower (and still are) than in Manhattan. She found a nursing job at City of Hope and rode the bus to work until she passed her driving exam. Near our apartment, dotting the way to my new school, were rows and rows of identical houses with pristine little lawns and fruit trees and rose bushes. There was one yard in particular, tended by a craggly witch of an old woman. She could often be seen in her yard, in her fluorescent, flower-patterned housecoat, with clippers in hand. Her face framed in silver, medusa-like ringlets, she rarely smiled, except while gazing on her flowers.

One day I made the mistake of asking her if I could pick some of her roses because it was Mother's Day. I knew I had no money to buy a gift. The old woman shook her clippers at me and said she'd been tending her "prize-winning rose bushes for years"; she'd be "damned if some wetback kid was going to ruin them." I fixed her with my deadliest hate stare, turned to walk away, and muttered, "I flew here on Air India, stupid."

I am not known for having a hot temper; even today, in my thirties, the more angry I am, the more silent I become. Back then, I skulked down the street, forlorn that I would be empty-handed when my mother walked into the house that evening. I got home and found one of the many pairs of surgical scissors my mother had emptied out from the deep pockets of her nurse's uniform, and waited. When dusk descended, I mounted my Huffy bike with the striped burnt sienna and glitter banana seat, and rode around to the old woman's home, circling like a vulture, up and down the street. I parked my bike a few houses down, behind some bushes where I knew it would be safe.

Then I did the unthinkable. I crept up to the chain link fence and slowly chopped myself a large bouquet of home-grown, prize-winning roses. I hacked them and put them, one by one, into my big hooded sweatshirt. I silently applied an inordinate amount of pressure to the scissors (surgical scissors are bad for trimming bushes or indeed any garden work), making deep red indentations on my index finger. I kept one eye on the window of the witch's living room. I could hear the faint voice of a male newscaster named Pat something as he announced the beginning of *Eye on LA.* I saw her stir in her Lazyboy chair, coughing up a lung and reaching for a very large mason jar with liquid in it. I was so hyper-alert that I could hear the ice in her drink clink against the glass. I ducked. Then I continued my thievery.

My small hands were covered in thorns by this time, the bad karma for my crime already taking its effect. I tried to cut off one final long, thick, red rose from the corner bush, so big and luscious was its head that I had to have it. I could not cut through the stem and began to open and close the scissors around it, making a butchered, fibrous mess of the stem. The more I did this, the more the scissors stuck, and the more I kept at it. I heard her stir, and then I heard the glass from which she was drinking crash to the ground and her scratchy voice whine, "Aww, shit." This is precisely what I was thinking just about then. As I saw her heave herself out of the chair, I gave the branch one last tug, and to my shock out came the whole bush, roots and all. While she was busy searching for a mop, my heart raced, beating loudly in my chest, pushing itself, lub dub, lub dub, against all the contraband flora inside my sweatshirt. I broke off the stem with my bare hands at this point, wincing at the pain caused by what seemed to be a thousand thorns. Crouching, I crawled down the street like a crab scuttling back into its hole. I found my bike. I leapt onto it like the Lone Ranger onto his horse, and rode toward the pink and violet, smog-streaked horizon.

I had less than 15 minutes before my mother would disembark from her bus and walk the two blocks to our doorstep. If I was lucky she might stop at the store to buy some milk, but that would take only another five minutes or so. I dumped all the roses into the sink, removed and threw my muddy sweatshirt into the hamper, and washed my hands, trying to pull the thorn pieces out of my bloody fingertips. When I looked into the medicine cabinet mirror, I saw tiny, red, livid scratches all over my chin, neck, and collarbone, and then hot, stinging tears rolled down my cheeks. I was horrified. It looked like I had tried to drown a cat. I didn't know what to do. I knew I had by now less than 10 minutes, and so I raced around the house, found several vases, filled them with water, and shoved the roses into them.

I put one on the dining table with the card I'd made in school, the other on the coffee table, and the other two by her bed and in the bathroom. I cleaned up the extra leaves, and as I heard the keys jingle in the door, felt an alarm go off in my head. I leapt into bed, pulling the covers over my head and switching the light off just as I heard her purse hit the table. "Wow, Pads!" I heard her singsong as she came down the hall. "These are great. Where'd you steal these from?"

# ROSE PETAL AND PISTACHIO ICE CREAM

Every time I treat myself to flowers or decorate my table with strewn fresh rose petals, I think of the rose witch and how I must have given her a heart attack the next day. I avoided that street for months, taking an alternate route to school until we finally moved. My mother was surprisingly pretty cool about it all and soon after started paying me an allowance for various household chores. I always felt I should have sent the old woman some flowers, but I don't remember the address, and by my account she would be 119 years old by now, for she was already at least 100 then.

2 cups heavy cream
2 cups whole milk
4 large egg yolks
½ cup sugar
1 teaspoon vanilla extract
2 tablespoons rose syrup *
5 tablespoons Turkish rose jam *
¼ cup crushed raw pistachios
2 tablespoons dried rose petals, without stems
    or leaves, just petals

**1** Heat the cream and milk over medium heat for 5 to 8 minutes, until the mixture almost boils.

**2** In a bowl, beat together the egg yolks, sugar, and vanilla extract until the mixture is smooth.

**3** Add 4 tablespoons of the hot cream mixture to the egg yolk mixture, stirring so the eggs won't curdle when heated.

**4** Reduce the heat to low, and gradually add the remaining egg yolk mixture to the cream and milk, being careful to prevent curdling of the eggs by continuously stirring. Cook for 3 to 5 minutes, until the mixture has thickened slightly. Stir in the rose syrup and rose jam. Cool the mixture completely, either overnight in the refrigerator or in an ice-water bath for 30 minutes.

**5** Pour the cooled cream into your ice cream maker and follow the manufacturer's instructions. When finished churning, remove the ice cream and fold in the pistachios and rose petals, mixing well to distribute evenly. Place the ice cream in the freezer for at least 6 to 8 hours (the rose syrup requires a longer freezing time) to solidify properly. **SERVES 6**

**NOTE** Both rose syrup and Turkish rose jam are available in gourmet and Middle Eastern markets as are organic dried rose petals. If you want a more delicately scented ice cream, you can use just the jam, but it's the syrup that gives this ice cream its rosy color.

# ORANGE BLOSSOM WAFFLES

We've all gotten so used to popping frozen waffles in the toaster that we forget the pleasure that comes from making waffles from scratch. And it's pretty easy. Use a hand mixer to get nice, stiff egg whites, and make sure the melted butter is cooled; that way it won't cook the other ingredients with its heat. As an alternative to maple syrup, I sometimes just melt some fruit jam or preserves in a small saucepan over low heat. You can add a bit of liqueur to this as well. For peach or apricot, I'd use Muscat; for orange marmalade, a brandy or calvados goes nicely; and Chambord pairs well with berry preserves. It's an easy way to make something new and to surprise whomever you're cooking for.

4 large eggs, separated
2 cups whole milk
½ cup melted butter, cooled
1 teaspoon vanilla extract
2 cups flour
2 teaspoons baking powder
1 teaspoon baking soda
1 tablespoon sugar
½ teaspoon salt
½ teaspoon ground cinnamon
½ teaspoon grated fresh nutmeg
3 tablespoons orange blossom water
    confectioners' sugar

**1** In a bowl, beat the egg yolks, and then add the milk, cooled melted butter, and vanilla.

**2** Sift together the flour, baking powder, baking soda, sugar, salt, cinnamon, and nutmeg.

**3** Gradually add the dry ingredients to the egg mixture and beat well.

**4** Separately, beat the egg whites until stiff. Carefully fold the whites into the batter, and then beat in the orange blossom water.

**5** Using a Belgian waffle iron and per the manufacturer's directions, cook the waffles.

**6** Dust with sifted confectioners' sugar, tapping and pushing it through a sieve with the back of a spoon. Serve with honey, maple syrup, or preserved fruit sauce. SERVES 4–6

# DRINKS

## HOMEMADE HOT CHOCOLATE

Ah, the joys of winter: sledding down the hill, having snowball fights with the neighbors, building snowmen, making snow angels on the lawn. Ah, the other joys of winter: shoveling the driveway, hauling in the Christmas tree, hauling out the Christmas tree, putting up the lights, taking down the lights, endless senseless shopping, etc., etc., etc. Wouldn't all of these tasks be just a bit more enriched by a steaming cup of hot chocolate?

5 cups whole milk
4 heaping teaspoons pure unsweetened Dutch-
    processed cocoa powder
3 ounces bittersweet or semisweet chocolate
    vanilla powder or a few drops of vanilla extract
    ground cinnamon

**1** In a large saucepan, gently heat the milk on medium to low heat. Add the cocoa powder spoon by spoon, mixing each into the milk before you add the next.

**2** With a flat cheese grater, shred the chocolate into the milk. Stir to blend the ingredients as you go. Add a pinch each of cinnamon and vanilla powder, or a few drops of vanilla extract.

**3** Simmer on low heat for 10 minutes. Serve piping hot in your favorite mugs. SERVES 4

## RASPBERRY CHAMPAGNE SPRITZER

This is one of my favorite party cocktails, one that I can't help but slurp up by the barrelful. And I guess if you were a teetotaler you could even make it with sparkling cider, but why would you want to do a virtuous thing like that?

6 strawberries, diced, plus 8 beautiful whole
    strawberries for garnishing
6 tablespoons raspberry sorbet
15 mint leaves, torn apart
1 bottle brut Champagne or Prosecco

**1** Slice the whole strawberries vertically just halfway up to the crown. Set these aside to use as garnish.

**2** Just before serving, place a tablespoon of sorbet in the bottom of a champagne flute. Place the mint leaves and some chopped strawberries in the glass, and pour in the champagne, being careful not to fill it so much that it froths over.

**3** Garnish the rim of each glass with the vertically sliced whole strawberry and serve immediately. SERVES 4–6

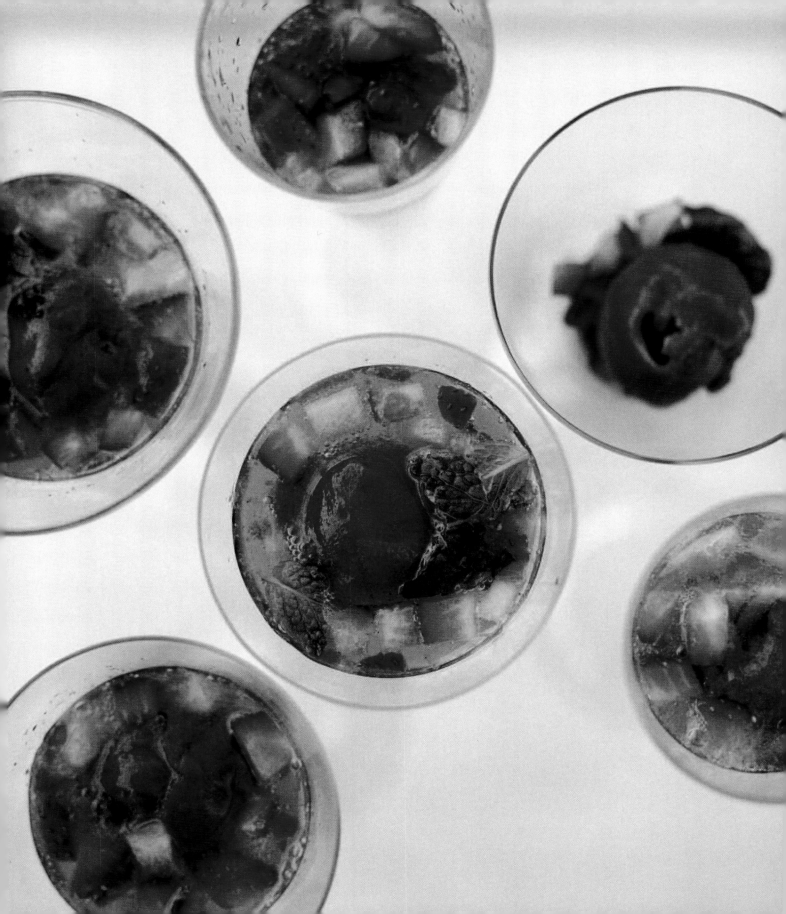

## HOMEMADE MASALA CHAI

A few years ago, I started to notice that my friends suddenly started using the word chai for tea and not because they had recently taken a trip to India or Russia. By now we are all familiar with Starbucks's chai lattes. But wouldn't it be nice to make homemade, ginger-steeped chai in your own kitchen once in a while ? This is a gorgeous way to finish a meal, and it's lovely to have a pot of it simmering on your kitchen stove for teatime. Make sure to buy a good variety of black tea, like Assam or Darjeeling. If you happen to be in an Indian grocery, ask them for Brook Bond or Red Label.

1 teaspoon finely diced fresh ginger
¼ teaspoon cardamom powder
¼ teaspoon ground cloves
3 teaspoons loose Darjeeling tea or other strong
   black tea
3 teaspoons brown sugar
1 cup whole milk
2 teaspoons honey

**1** In a saucepan, bring the ginger, cardamom, and cloves to a boil with 4 cups of water. Reduce the heat to a simmer and add the tea, sugar, milk, and honey. Simmer 2 to 3 minutes while stirring to dissolve the sugar. Strain the tea into cups and serve hot. SERVES 4

## A COMFORTING LEMONADE

Oh, how a gentle breeze runs through my hair and kicks up my petticoat as I sit in the swing on my imaginary wraparound porch. I am at times a frustrated Southern Belle in the most American sense of the word. Mind you, gals from South India are a whole 'nother bag, but I digress. This is a joyous way to enjoy a spiked lemonade on a hot summer evening. Be careful not to fall off your swing, as this tends to be a common side effect of gulping down one too many tall glasses of this tawny potation.

4 tablespoons sugar
½ cup fresh-squeezed lemon juice
   juice of 1 lime
1 cup whole cherries, halved and pitted
3 or 4 mint leaves, torn into bits
1 ½ cups Southern Comfort whiskey

**1** Warm 2 cups of water over medium-low heat and mix in the sugar, dissolving it completely.

**2** In a pitcher, place—in this order—the lemon and lime juices, the sugar water, 4 cups of water, the cherries, the mint leaves, 1 cup of ice, and finally the whiskey. Stir. Serve immediately. SERVES 4–6

## WHITE SANGRIA

This is a light, pleasing sangria that pairs well with fish and chicken. You can use fresh pineapple, but, frankly, canned is just fine. I can't wait to get it all mixed up and poured into a glass so I can beat it out to my lawn chair faster than you can say, "Buenos dias!"

3 3-inch-long cinnamon sticks
1 8-ounce can pineapple rings, cut into pieces
2 kiwis, peeled and sliced
1 mango, ripe but still firm, peeled, pitted, and
  cubed
5 whole star anise pods
1 750-ml bottle Spanish white wine
1 cup peach liqueur

Toss together the cinnamon, fruit, and star anise, and place the mixture in a pitcher. Pour in liqueur and wine and combine. Let the sangria sit in the fridge for at least 2 to 3 hours and serve cold. If desired, add ice before serving. SERVES 4–6

# PICK-
# LES
# AND
# CHUT-
# NEYS

## GREEN APPLE AND MINT CHUTNEY

This glorious green chutney is blended fresh and will keep for a couple of days in your fridge. It's great with fish and even poached shrimp or as a dip for kabobs. I have more than once managed to put away, in one sitting, a whole bag of chips dipped in this chutney because its call to me from the fridge was too much to resist. The hot serrano chilies are tempered by the cool tingle of fresh mint. The apples, of course, make the taste buds sing. Keep this chilled, if there happens to be anything leftover.

1 Granny Smith apple, cored and cut into
   16 pieces
3 cups loosely packed fresh mint leaves
4 serrano or Thai green chilies, coarsely chopped
   with seeds
2 cups loosely packed fresh cilantro
1 medium tomato, chunked with juices and seeds
   salt
2 tablespoons fresh-squeezed lemon juice

Put all the ingredients except the salt in a blender or food processor, and puree until smooth. Remove from the blender; add the salt. Stir the chutney well and store it in the refrigerator, where it will keep for 4 or 5 days. MAKES 4–5 CUPS

## FRESH MINT CHUTNEY

You will find a million uses for this simple dipping sauce, including whisking a bit into salad dressings and mixing it with yogurt for a thicker dip. It's best with anything fried. Even eggs get a grassy coat of glamour from this chutney.

2 ½ cups fresh mint leaves
1 serrano or Thai chili
2 tablespoons fresh-squeezed lemon juice
½ teaspoon sugar
    salt

Combine all the ingredients in a blender. A tablespoon of water or 2 can be added to help blend the ingredients, if needed. Pack the sauce in a jar, cover it with its lid, and store it in the refrigerator, where it will keep for 2–3 days. **MAKES ABOUT 3 CUPS**

## FRESH MINT AND DATE DIPPING SAUCE

This is a variation on the classic mint chutney from above, and one worth whipping up. The dates impart a bit of sticky sweetness that is divine when mixed with the fire of these green chilies. I've even served it spooned over some sliced roast pork and it's out of this world. You may need a bit of water to blend all the ingredients but add a little at a time, because you don't want it too be too watery. You can make it ahead of serving too as it lasts for a few days in the fridge.

2 cups fresh mint leaves
3 dried dates, pitted
5 serrano chilies, stem removed.
2 tablespoons freshly squeezed lemon juice

Put all the ingredients in a blender or processor and puree to form a smooth uniform dipping sauce. Will keep for 2–3 days in the fridge. **MAKES ABOUT 2 ½ CUPS**

# LEMON PICKLE

This is a classic recipe for a puckering, hot pickle that is great as a relish for meats and can be spread into sandwiches. In India, this traditional condiment would be served with every meal. You can also fling a dollop of it into the pan while making home fries, sautéing any vegetable, or pan-searing a fish fillet. It does require some planning ahead as the lemon takes 6 months to pickle.

6 lemons
6 tablespoons coarse rock salt
2–3 tablespoons canola oil
5 big black cardamom pods
3 heaping teaspoons cayenne
1 teaspoon turmeric
½ teaspoon asafetida powder
½ teaspoon black peppercorns
½ teaspoon anise seed
½ teaspoon cumin seeds

**1** Cut the lemons into chunks, place them in a glass canning jar, and cover them with the rock salt. Store the jar for 6 months in a dark pantry cupboard.

**2** Heat the oil in a large frying pan. Using a mortar and pestle or a coffee grinder, grind all the remaining ingredients to form a coarse powder. Now add the powder to the hot oil. Stir this mixture over medium heat for 12 minutes. Remove it from the heat and let it cool.

**3** Add the lemon and salt mixture to the spices and stir well. Keep this pickle in an airtight glass jar, where it will last for up to a year. **MAKES ABOUT 2 CUPS**

# TOMATO CHUTNEY

I know this recipe calls for a long list of ingredients, but by now you should be familiar with most of them. Also, this is such a traditional chutney recipe that I felt you should at least know about it. It will keep in your fridge for a few days and can even be frozen so you would have to make a big batch of it only two or three times a year. Oh, come on, just try it. It goes great with chips, flatbread, and any of the other things you would normally use salsa for. I've even swirled it into noodle soup to spice things up. If you don't have the white gram lentils, don't fret; just use some peanuts or cashews, or skip them altogether.

1 tablespoon sesame seeds
1 tablespoon fenugreek seeds
1 tablespoon coriander seeds
1 tablespoon white gram lentils
1 pound tomatoes, chopped
1 ounce (golf-ball size) knob of tamarind pulp,
   soaked in a cup of boiling water (see page 63)
10 red whole dry chilies
¼ cup sesame oil
1 teaspoon black mustard seeds
1 teaspoon asafetida powder
½ teaspoon turmeric powder

**1** In a skillet, dry-roast the sesame, fenugreek, and coriander seeds, along with the white gram lentils, over medium heat for a few minutes, stirring to cook all evenly.

**2** In a food processor or blender, blend together the tomatoes, tamarind gravy, and red chilies to create a puree.

**3** In another small skillet, heat the oil and cook the mustard seeds until they begin to pop and crackle. Add the asafetida. Now add the tomato puree and the turmeric powder. Cook for 8 minutes or until the oil separates into small pools on top. Add the powdered, dry-roasted spices, and continue to heat to reduce the sauce to a thick chutney, about 7–10 more minutes.
MAKES ABOUT 3½–4 CUPS

## FRANCESCO CLEMENTE'S AMAZING HOT SAUCE (CHIPOTLE & DATE CHUTNEY)

This hot sauce is named after my very dear friend, Francesco. I always joke that Francesco is really an Indian man trapped in an Italian body, and he tells me I am really an Italian trapped in an Indian body. He and his beautiful and elegant wife lived in Madras when I was very young. He is now so addicted to this sauce that I feel like a drug dealer when he calls to say he's finished his stash. With four children, he is forced to hide it deep in the back of the fridge. I love the tastes of hot and sweet in the same bite, as you may have figured out by now. And I love the tear-inducing fieriness of pickled chipotle peppers. My favorite brand, La Morena, comes in a bright orange can. This condiment will keep nicely in the fridge for a couple of months.

10 fresh or dried dates, pitted, cut into chunks
4 plum tomatoes, seeded, with the juice squeezed
  from them
13 ounces pickled chipotle peppers in adobo
  sauce
2 cloves garlic
⅓ cup honey
1 teaspoon coarse sea salt

In a blender or processor, combine all the ingredients and blend until they make a thick paste. Pour into a deep saucepan, and cook over medium-low heat for about 5 to 6 minutes, adding ¼ cup of water halfway through and stirring. Cool and then store in an airtight glass jar.
**MAKES ABOUT 3½–4 CUPS**

# TANGERINE PEEL PICKLE

Now I will forewarn you that there may be a few ingredients like asafetida powder and fenugreek that may not already be in your larder, but you can get all these at your local Indian store, or mail order them from Kalustyan's in New York, and my good friend Aziz will ship them anywhere. These ingredients don't cost very much at all, and I promise you this pickle is worth it. I spread it on sandwiches, sauté fish fillets on the fly by flinging a dollop of this pickle into the pan, and even stir it into some sour cream for an interesting dip. My grandmother first taught me how to make it years ago and it remains one of my favorite condiments.

2 ½ tablespoons canola oil
½ teaspoon black mustard seeds
¼ teaspoon asafetida powder
    peel of 6 tangerines, cut in slivers
1 tablespoon minced fresh ginger
3 fresh Thai green chilies or serrano or jalapeño
    chilies
1 teaspoon dry-roasted fenugreek seeds
1 teaspoon urad lentils
1 teaspoon sesame seeds
2 teaspoons turmeric powder
1 cup tamarind gravy (made from 1 ounce dried
    tamarind soaked in 1 cup boiling water for
    20 minutes, then strained; see page 66)
    salt
1-inch cube of jaggery (brown cane sugar or
    palm sugar)

**1** Heat the oil in a large skillet over medium heat. Add the mustard seeds; when they start to crackle and pop, stir in the asafetida powder. Add the tangerine peel, ginger, and green chilies; stir-fry for 7–8 minutes, reducing the heat to medium low.

**2** Dry-roast the fenugreek seeds, urad lentils, and sesame seeds in a dry, hot frying pan, with no oil, on medium-high heat on top of the stove for 3 minutes, stirring constantly so they cook evenly. When they darken to a light toasted brown, place them in a mortar, and grind them vigorously into a powder with a pestle.

**3** Add the turmeric, tamarind gravy, and salt to the skillet with the peels. Bring to a slow boil, raising the heat slightly, and add the jaggery, stirring to dissolve it into the mixture.

**4** Add the powdered, dry-roasted mixture to the skillet. Reduce the heat and cook the pickle down until it becomes a sticky paste, stirring often to prevent it sticking on the bottom of the pan. Store in an airtight glass jar in the fridge. It will keep for about a week to 10 days. You can serve this pickle with grilled fish or roasted chicken, or even mix it into hot, plain rice for a quick pilaf. MAKES ABOUT 1½ CUPS

# CRANBERRY CHUTNEY

My sweet great-aunt Bala used to make this chutney every year at Thanksgiving, and I must say it saved many a turkey sandwich from pathetic dullness. In college, I mixed it into boiled rice for a quick pilaf and smeared it on flatbreads with meat inside to make Indian kaati rolls (what we now call wraps). Aunt Bala was a fantastic cook who moved to the States after retirement to live with her son, my Uncle Vichu. I always admired how Bala incorporated the strange, new fruits of her adopted country into her culinary repertoire. This is a very spicy, Indian-tasting chutney made with a very American fruit.

4 tablespoons canola oil
24 ounces cranberries, fresh or frozen *
3 tablespoons sugar
1 teaspoon cayenne
  salt
½ teaspoon fenugreek seeds
½ teaspoon asafetida powder
½ teaspoon tumeric powder

**1** Heat the oil on medium heat and sauté the cranberries, stirring intermittently. The entire process should take 1½ to 2 hours; the cranberries should open gradually and then begin to burst.

**2** After about 45 minutes, add the sugar, cayenne, and salt. Adjust the heat to medium low, stirring all the ingredients.

**3** Place the fenugreek in a dry skillet and roast for a few minutes. Grind to a powder in a mortar with a pestle. Combine with the asafetida and tumeric.

**4** When the cranberries have cooked for about 1¼ hours, add the ground powders and continue to cook. The chutney should be ready when the cranberries have burst and the mixture is a thick, bubbling paste. This chutney will keep for months in a airtight glass jar in the fridge.
**MAKES ABOUT 2½ CUPS**

**NOTE** If you use frozen cranberries, make the following adjustments: First, thaw the cranberries. Heat the oil on medium heat and sauté the cranberries, stirring intermittently. This process is much speedier and should take a total of only 30–40 minutes, with the end result a thick paste. Add the cayenne and salt halfway through cooking, and the sugar and asafetida and fenugreek powder about 5 minutes later (about 20 minutes into cooking). The chutney should be ready when the cranberries have burst and the mixture is a thick paste.

## CHILI HONEY BUTTER

Chili . . . honey . . . butter. Need I say more? It's actually dangerous to keep this condiment around because you will find yourself buttering your toast with it, frying up eggs with a bit of it melted in the pan, not to mention making home fries, too. And that's just breakfast. It can be used to sauté green beans and carrots, to brush on grilled fish, even to baste a whole chicken for roasting. The possibilities are endless (see, for example, the Barbeque Shrimp with Chili Honey Butter recipe, on page 86).

8 tablespoons (1 stick) unsalted butter, at room
   temperature
1 ½ tablespoons honey
1 teaspoon cayenne
   salt

Combine all the ingredients and whip in a blender or processor or just by hand with a fork until they form a smooth sauce. Spoon it into a rigid plastic container and keep covered in the fridge. MAKES ABOUT 1 CUP

# RECIPE INDEX

UNIFEM EVENT
17 NOV. 2004

NAME/DEPT.

DATE:

Issuing Officer

FAJMA
F          USA
SEPT 70

INSERT THIS SI

OLIVE OIL

زيت زيتون خضير الكشرا

شعيفان

KOURA الكورة
SAIFAN
EXTRA VIRGIN OLIVE OIL

Packed by: SAID SAIFAN EST.